Reader's Digest Needlecraft Guides

EMBROIDERY

Reader's Digest Needlecraft Guides

EMBROIDERY

Step-by-step instructions for over 75 stitches

Published by The Reader's Digest Association Limited
LONDON • NEW YORK • SYDNEY • CAPETOWN • MONTREAL

READER'S DIGEST NEEDLECRAFT GUIDE: EMBROIDERY
First published 1995
Copyright © Text and Illustrations 1995, 1981

The material in this book first appeared in
READER'S DIGEST COMPLETE GUIDE TO NEEDLEWORK
First edition Copyright © 1981
Reprinted 1991
The Reader's Digest Association Limited,
Berkeley Square House, Berkeley Square, London W1X 6AB

Copyright © 1981 Reader's Digest Association Far East Limited
Philippines Copyright 1981 Reader's Digest Association Far East Ltd

Printed in Italy

ISBN 0 2764 2178 7

CONTRIBUTORS

The publishers would like to thank the following people for major contributions to this series.

Consultant editor Eirian Short

Editorial contributors and designers

Louise Amble   Peggy Bendel   Sherry De Leon   Rosemary Drysdale   Katherine Enzmann   Phoebe Fox   Zuelia Ann Hurt
Barbara H. Jacksier   Joyce D. Lee   Susanna E. Lewis   Claudia Librett   Victoria Mileti   Edna Adam Walker
Monna Weinman   Joanne Whitwell

Technical assistance

Elspeth Arnold   Lesley Arnold   Betty Beeby   Linda Blyer   Barbara Dawson   Janet Eaton   Charlotte Feng-Veshi
Sheila Gore   Jane Iles   Diana Keay   Elizabeth Kerr   Arlene Mintzer   Carole Nolan   Erwin Rowland
Cathie Strunz   Valentina Watson   Joan Webb

Contributing artists

Roberta W. Frauwirth   Susan Frye   Pat Kemmish   John A. Lind Corp.   Marilyn MacGregor   Mary Ruth Roby   Jim Silks
Randall Lieu   Ray Skibinski   Lynn E. Yost

Contributing photographers

J. D. Barnell   Bruton Photography   Joel Elkins   Ken Korsh   Ross McCann/Conrad-Dell-McCrann, Inc.   Michael A. Vaccaro

Research assistance

Aero Needles (Abel Morrall)   Appletons Bros Ltd   C. J. Bates & Son   Emile Bernat & Sons Co.   Bernina Sewing Machines
Boye Needle Company   Brunswick Worsted Mills Inc.   J. & P. Coats   Cowling & Wilcox   Craftsman's Mark
The D.M.C. Corporation   Embroiderers' Guild   Frederick J. Fawcett Inc.   T. Forsell & Son   Harrods Ltd
Harry M. Fraser Company   Hayfield Textiles   Hosiery Machine Co.   Kreinik Mfg Co.   Lowe & Carr   H. Milward & Sons
Newey Goodman   Paternayan Bros Inc.   Paton & Baldwins   Phildar International   Pingouin   Reynolds Yarn Inc.
Royal School of Needlework   Singer Company (UK) Ltd   Sirdar   Talon/Donahue Sales Div. of Textron   Joan Toggitt Ltd
Twilleys of Stamford   Vilene   Whitecroft Scovill   Wm. E. Wright Co.

Cover

Photography by Paul Biddle   Craftwork supplied by Dora Lockyer

Embroidery

Nineteenth-century bedspread with crewel-work embroidery, Historic Deerfield Inc., Deerfield, Mass.

Embroidery tools and supplies

Yarns and threads

Embroidery offers an enormous variety of finished effects, and that calls for a wide range of yarns and threads. Several of the types popular for embroidery are pictured below. Although they differ individually in texture, fibre content, number of plies, separable strands, etc., all of the types shown have one feature in common: whatever their character, it remains uniform throughout. Uneven or knobbly novelty yarns are generally not recommended for embroidery, except for occasional special effects.

Some yarns and threads come in more than one fibre, with new ones constantly being introduced, especially synthetic varieties. Some yarns and threads are easier to find than others; you may need to check several sources – needlework departments as well as special shops and catalogues – to find what you want.

In this section, as each form of embroidery is introduced, we specify the yarn or thread traditional for working it. This should not discourage experiment with different yarns and threads – that is what produces original pieces.

Embroidery floss, a loosely twisted 6-strand thread, works well in many types of embroidery. Strands can be separated for finer work. Cotton is most popular; made also in silk and rayon. Many colours (fewer for rayon).

Pearl cotton, a twisted 2-ply thread suitable for all embroidery types, has high sheen, good colours. Comes in sizes 3, 5, and 8 (3 is the heaviest).

Matte embroidery cotton, a tightly twisted 5-ply thread, gives embroidery a muted look. Usually reserved for heavier fabrics. Good colour choice.

Crewel yarn, of fine 2-ply wool (also some acrylic), resembles one strand of Persian yarn. For fine embroidery and needlepoint. Many soft, subtle colours.

Persian yarn is loosely twisted 3-strand wool (sometimes acrylic); each strand is 2-ply. Used in needlepoint and embroidery. Good colour choice.

Tapestry yarn is a tightly twisted 4-ply yarn appropriate for embroidery and needlepoint. Choice of wool (in many colours) or acrylic (considerably fewer).

Knitting yarn is a 4-ply yarn, like tapestry yarn but less twisted. Usable also for crochet. May be wool or acrylic.

Rug yarn, a thick 3-ply yarn, can also be used for texture variation in embroidered pieces; works best when it is couched down (fastened with small stitches). May be wool, acrylic, or cotton/rayon blend.

Machine embroidery thread is extra fine (size 50 or A). Silk is most popular for its sheen.

Metallic threads, available in many weights and textures, are used only for special effects.

Embroidery fabrics

Embroidery fabrics fall basically into three categories. The first, **plain-weave fabrics,** includes most tightly woven fabrics with a relatively smooth surface. Although medium-weight linens and wools are the traditional preferences, fabrics of other weights and fibres (such as cotton and synthetics) are also acceptable as long as the working thread is not too heavy. Most surface stitchery (including crewel work) is worked on plain-weave fabrics.

Even-weave fabrics, the next of the classifications, are all essentially plain weaves, but with a distinguishing difference: the number of threads per square centimetre is the same for both warp and weft. One type, the *single even-weave,* is made from single strands of intersecting threads; the thread count can vary from a coarse 6 to a fine 14 threads per square centimetre. In *Hardanger,* another of the even-weave types, pairs of threads intersect; 9 pairs of threads per centimetre is the usual count. Still another type is *Binca cloth,* which consists of intersecting thread groups, generally 4 to the centimetre. As a rule, even-weave fabrics are used for thread-counting techniques, such as blackwork and some types of openwork. They may be cotton, linen, wool, or blends of these with synthetics.

What the fabrics in the third group have in common is an evenly spaced **surface pattern** (see examples on right) that supplies guidelines for certain kinds of embroidery, such as cross stitch and smocking. As the samples show, the surface pattern may be printed on or woven in. The method of producing the effect is not important; what matters is its usefulness as a grid. The fabric *type,* however, is important. Select woven fabrics for this purpose; knitted fabrics are rarely satisfactory.

This list of embroidery fabrics is far from complete – silk, damask fabrics and calico, among others, may be used.

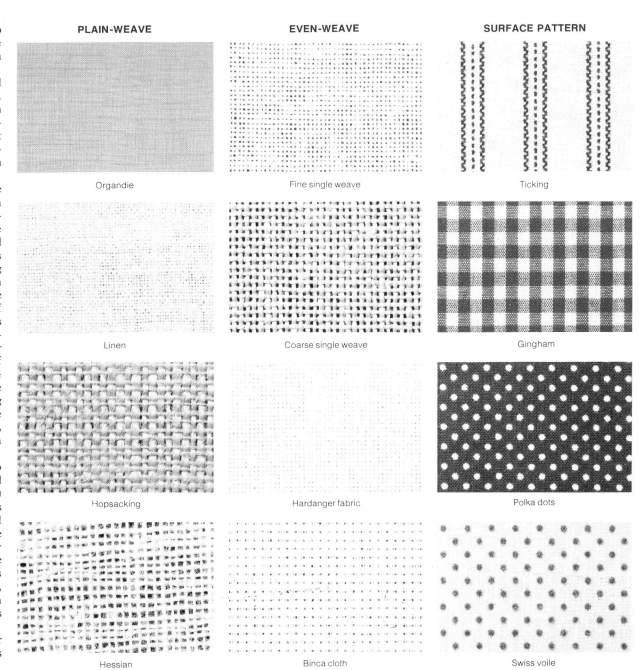

PLAIN-WEAVE

Organdie

Linen

Hopsacking

Hessian

EVEN-WEAVE

Fine single weave

Coarse single weave

Hardanger fabric

Binca cloth

SURFACE PATTERN

Ticking

Gingham

Polka dots

Swiss voile

Embroidery tools and materials

Hoops and frames

A hoop or frame is necessary for most types of embroidery work, to hold the fabric taut for stitching. **Embroidery hoops** keep a section of fabric stretched between two rings. The outer ring usually has an adjustable screw or a spring that allows the hoop to hold different weights of fabric. Hoops come in many sizes and may be hand-held or attached to a stand. **Frames** work by keeping the entire fabric taut. There are two basic types, the slate or square frame and the stretcher frame. *Slate frames* stretch the fabric between top and bottom rollers, which are then tightened. On the *stretcher frames*, which are basically four-sided units that you make with pre-cut wooden slats, the fabric is very firmly stretched around the framework and then neatly stapled down all around the back.

Needles

Needles for hand embroidery are of three basic types: **crewel, chenille** and **tapestry**. Each has a specific purpose and comes in its own range of sizes (the larger the number, the shorter and finer the needle). Which needle type you should use depends largely on the embroidery technique being worked (see below). Another consideration is the thread; the needle should be large enough that the thread does not fray when it is pulled through the fabric.

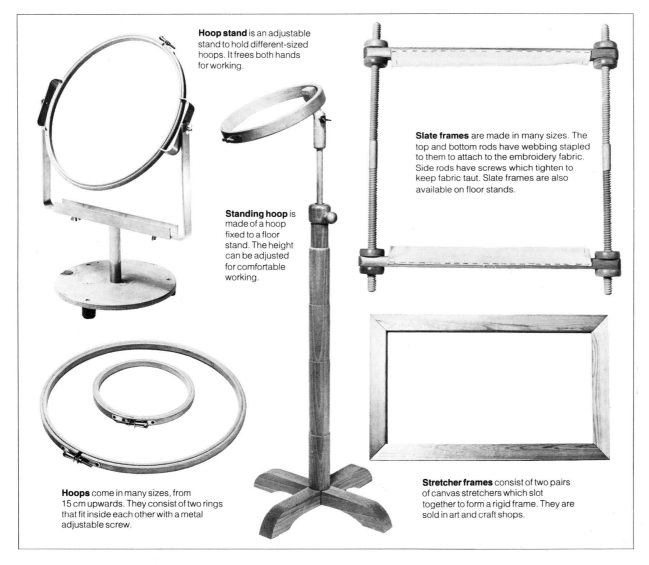

Hoop stand is an adjustable stand to hold different-sized hoops. It frees both hands for working.

Standing hoop is made of a hoop fixed to a floor stand. The height can be adjusted for comfortable working.

Slate frames are made in many sizes. The top and bottom rods have webbing stapled to them to attach to the embroidery fabric. Side rods have screws which tighten to keep fabric taut. Slate frames are also available on floor stands.

Hoops come in many sizes, from 15 cm upwards. They consist of two rings that fit inside each other with a metal adjustable screw.

Stretcher frames consist of two pairs of canvas stretchers which slot together to form a rigid frame. They are sold in art and craft shops.

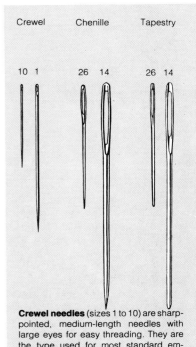

Crewel		Chenille		Tapestry	
10	1	26	14	26	14

Crewel needles (sizes 1 to 10) are sharp-pointed, medium-length needles with large eyes for easy threading. They are the type used for most standard embroidery stitchery.
Chenille needles (sizes 14 to 26) are also sharp-pointed needles, but they are thicker and longer, and have larger eyes. They are the appropriate choice for embroidery using heavier threads.
Tapestry needles (sizes 14 to 26) are similar in size to chenille needles, but are blunt rather than sharp. This makes them best for thread-counting embroidery techniques and for canvas work as well.

Design transfer materials

Dressmaker's carbon paper and tracing wheels are used to transfer designs to fabric. Carbon paper is available in a few colours.

Pounce, sometimes called 'inking' powder, is used to transfer designs by the pricking method.

Dressmaker's marking pencils are used to mark fabric, will not smudge and are made in pale colours.

Transfer pencil enables you to make a hot-iron transfer from any design or drawing.

Tracing paper is useful for transferring original designs, and can be bought in many sizes.

Transfers are heat-sensitive patterns that can be ironed on to fabric. There are many types of design available.

Accessories

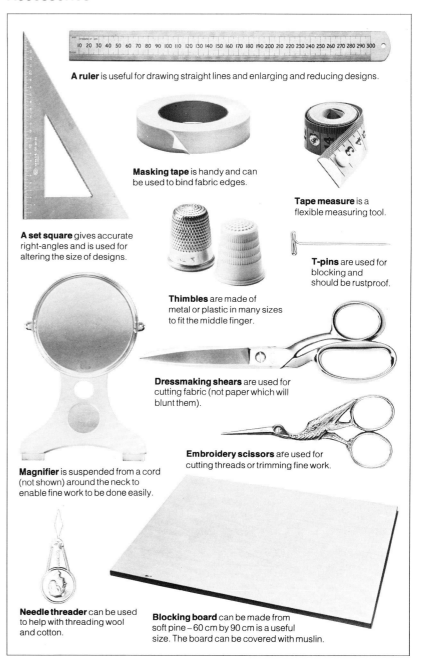

A ruler is useful for drawing straight lines and enlarging and reducing designs.

Masking tape is handy and can be used to bind fabric edges.

Tape measure is a flexible measuring tool.

A set square gives accurate right-angles and is used for altering the size of designs.

T-pins are used for blocking and should be rustproof.

Thimbles are made of metal or plastic in many sizes to fit the middle finger.

Dressmaking shears are used for cutting fabric (not paper which will blunt them).

Embroidery scissors are used for cutting threads or trimming fine work.

Magnifier is suspended from a cord (not shown) around the neck to enable fine work to be done easily.

Needle threader can be used to help with threading wool and cotton.

Blocking board can be made from soft pine – 60 cm by 90 cm is a useful size. The board can be covered with muslin.

9

Designing for embroidery

Sources and interpretation

Many needleworkers who have become quite skilled still do not consider themselves designers. Yet all of us, if we try, can manage some degree of designing. One person might take a first creative step by simply changing the thread colours dictated by a kit. Another may go a step further and make all of the colour and stitch decisions. Still another may carry out an original design. It is hoped that this section will encourage more people to try introducing their own ideas into their embroidery.

Many embroidery designs are nothing but personal interpretations of designs from such sources as books, magazines, posters, china, fabric prints, wallpaper and photographs. Examine such possible sources carefully, studying elements *within* a composition as well as the overall composition itself; you may find that you can single out a part of the larger design (see below) with excellent results. Take note of designs that draw the eye naturally up and down or from side to side. This can determine whether the overall line direction of a finished piece will be vertical or horizontal.

When you find a design that you like, place tracing paper over it, and carefully draw its outlines. You may want to omit some of the finer details, perhaps simplify certain lines as well; you can even rearrange elements within the composition. Make several different tracings and select the best one. Remember you are not trying to copy the original design, but to interpret it in embroidery. As you become more experienced at design interpretation, you will begin to recognise what has possibilities for embroidery and – just as important – what does not.

Part of a composition can be isolated for an embroidery design. From design below, bird and

flower have been singled out and traced, note the simplifications made in the tracing.

The strong horizontal lines in the full design direct the eye naturally to move from side to side.

Vertical lines draw the eye up and down

Choosing colours

Once your design is chosen, you are ready to select colours, a decision that will greatly affect your finished project. With colour, as with most design problems, there are guidelines that can help you to make a successful choice. Most colour schemes are one of three basic types. The first, called **monochromatic,** is a colour scheme consisting of different tones (light and dark hues) of the *same* colour (a design done in a 'family' of blues). The second type, the **analogous** colour scheme, uses colours that are *similar*, and 'neighbours' on the colour wheel (blues and greens or violets). A **contrasting** colour scheme, the third combination, brings together two or more *contrasting* colours, the strongest contrasts being those that are opposites on the colour wheel (red and green, purple and yellow).

These colour guidelines, though simple in theory, can be more difficult to put into practice. You will find the task far easier if you make yourself a *colour plan* – a coloured version of your traced design. You may have to colour more than one drawing before you hit upon a satisfactory combination. Once you have one you like, take it along when you go to buy threads. Be ready to make slight modifications in colours when you see what threads are actually available.

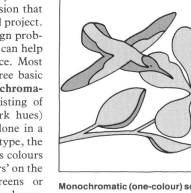  

Monochromatic (one-colour) schemes can achieve surprising variety if the tones (tints and shades) are imaginatively chosen and used, as illustrated.

 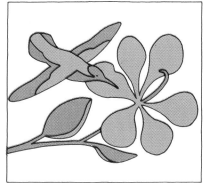 

Analogous schemes combine closely related colours, a characteristic that almost assures a harmonious blend, no matter what combination you choose.

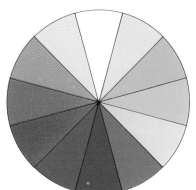

Colour wheel

  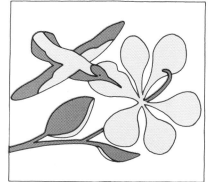

Contrasting schemes can be much more difficult. Experiment with several different colours until you are satisfied.

11

Designing for embroidery

Enlarging a design

What do you do if the design you like is not the right size for your project? If there is a commercial photostat service near by, you can give them your drawing or the original artwork and have the size changed to your specifications. The cost for this service is nominal. If there is no such service in your area, or you prefer to do it yourself, you can make your own size change, using the grid methods illustrated – enlargement on this page, reduction on the page opposite. Basically, this method involves simply transposing design lines from one grid to another grid of a different size.

1. Trace design on to centre of paper.

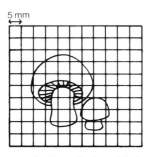
2. Draw a small grid over the traced design.

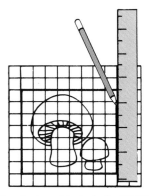
3. Mark perimeters of design to desired shape.

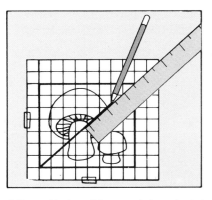
4. Tape grid to lower left corner of a large sheet of paper. Draw a corner-to-corner line diagonally across design area, extending line beyond grid.

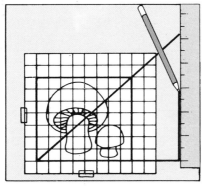
5. Extend the bottom line of the design area to desired width. Draw a line straight up to form a right-angle, extending line to intersect diagonal.

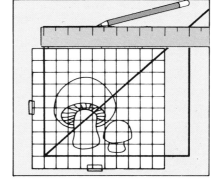
6. Using the finished width and height in Step 5, draw in remaining two sides of rectangle (left-hand line will join line of original grid).

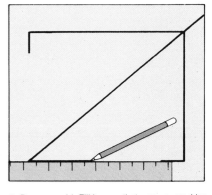
7. Remove grid. Fill in area that was covered by grid, extending diagonal, side and bottom lines to complete enlarged rectangle.

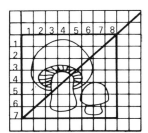
8. Along the design perimeter of the small grid, number each square across top and down side.

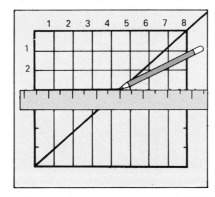
9. Count the squares within marked grid; divide large rectangle into same number of squares.

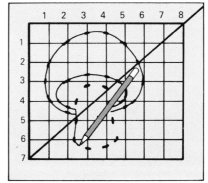
10. To reproduce design, copy lines in small squares on corresponding squares of large grid.

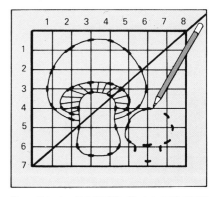
To make copying easier, place a mark where design lines intersect grid lines; connect marks.

5 mm

1 2 3 4 5 6 7 8

Reducing a design

When a design is too large, you have the same choices as when it is too small. It can be reduced to your specifications by a commercial photostat service, as mentioned on the opposite page, or you can reduce the design yourself, by means of the grid technique shown here. The basic principle – copying square by square – is the same for reducing as for enlarging, but the actual steps differ. Essentially, they are the reverse of what is done for enlargement. Follow directions carefully when using either method; for drawing accurate angles, use a plastic right-angled set-square.

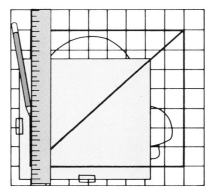

1. Trace design on to centre of paper.

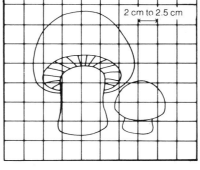

2. Draw large grid over traced design.

2 cm to 2.5 cm

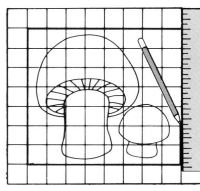

3. Mark perimeters of design to desired shape.

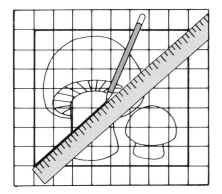

4. Draw a diagonal line from corner to corner of the design area marked off on the grid. Tape a smaller sheet of paper to the lower left corner.

5. Extend the diagonal line at the upper right-hand corner of the grid straight down to the lower left-hand corner of the taped sheet of paper.

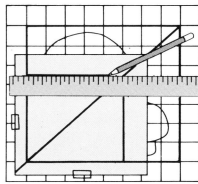

6. Extend bottom line of design area until it intersects diagonal. Connect intersected point with perimeter line on left side to form right-angle.

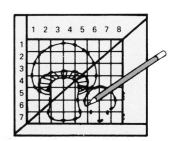

7. Mark off desired width at bottom of small sheet; draw line up at right-angle to intersect diagonal. Mark height on left; draw connecting line at top.

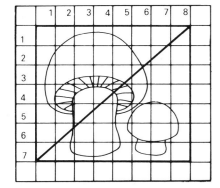

8. Along the design perimeter of the large grid, number each square across top and down side.

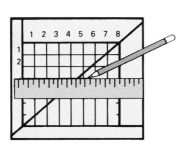

9. Count the number of squares within marked grid; divide small rectangle into same number.

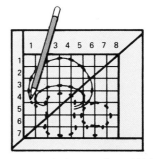

10. To reproduce design, copy lines within large squares on to equivalent squares of small grid.

To make copying easier, place a mark where design lines intersect grid lines; connect marks.

General embroidery techniques

Cutting and binding fabric edges
Transferring designs
Using an embroidery hoop
Preparing threads
Threading the needle
Working tips

Cutting and binding edges

To determine cutting size of fabric, measure the overall design and to this measurement add 5 cm all round. Add twice as much allowance if the embroidered piece is to be framed. Cut fabric to the desired size, following the fabric's grainline; a straight grain is especially important for counted-thread embroidery. To keep the fabric from fraying during any lengthy embroidering process, finish off the raw edges, using one of the methods shown below.

Use masking tape over raw edges of fabric.

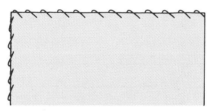

Overcast raw edges by hand to prevent fraying.

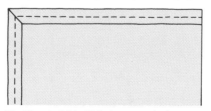

Machine straight-stitch along turned edges.

Machine zigzag raw edges for easy finish.

Transferring designs

Transfer of a design to a fabric can be accomplished by any of three different methods. The first, and probably the easiest, is to use a **hot-iron transfer**, which is simply a printed, heat-sensitive pattern. When the pattern is placed against the fabric and heat from an iron is applied, the design comes off on to the fabric. Commercial hot-iron transfers are produced in a variety of designs. Though most hot-iron transfers are good for only a single printing, there are some specially made to be used more than once. If you prefer to use a design of your own, you can make your own hot-iron transfer with a special transfer pencil (see opposite page).

Another method of design transfer involves the use of **dressmaker's carbon** and a tracing wheel. Do not confuse this type of carbon with typing carbon paper, which can smear badly. The method is basically the same as that used to transfer pattern markings in standard sewing procedures. Dressmaker's carbon is suitable for marking only very smooth fabrics.

Pouncing is one of the oldest and still an effective means of transferring a design. Little holes are pricked along the outline of the design pattern, which is then laid over the fabric and rubbed with *pounce powder*. This is available from artists' suppliers, and is sometimes known as 'inking' powder. When the pattern is lifted away, a fine dotted line remains on the fabric. The dotted lines are then drawn over with a dressmaker's pencil; on fabrics that cannot be pencilled (such as velvet), this step can be done with a fine paintbrush and opaque watercolours. The pricked patterns can be used more than once, and are especially suited to slightly textured fabrics. This method is also suitable for transferring quilting designs.

With all methods of transferring, be sure that the pattern design is properly placed on the fabric (see right).

PLACING DESIGN

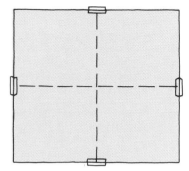

Fold and quarter fabric; crease along folds. If crease will not hold, tack centre foldlines. Pin or tape fabric to flat surface.

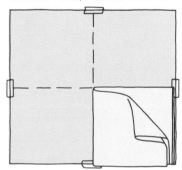

Fold and quarter pattern (design should be centred). Place pattern in one quarter of fabric, centre points aligned.

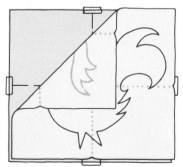

Carefully open out pattern so foldlines match crease lines of fabric. Anchor pattern down, then transfer design.

HOT-IRON TRANSFERS

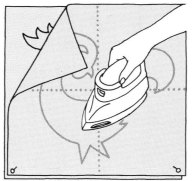

To make your own hot-iron transfer, copy design on heavy tracing paper. Turn paper to back and trace over lines with transfer pencil. With traced side down on fabric, press transfer as described on the right. A wax crayon can be used as a transfer pencil, but usually produces a thick line, so it is recommended only for large designs on coarse fabrics.

To use hot-iron transfer, first cut off any waste lettering and test on scrap of fabric. If test piece takes, position main transfer face down on fabric, and pin at corners. Turn iron to low setting and press down on transfer for a few seconds; lift, then move to next area. Do not glide iron over transfer. Lift up corner to make sure transfer is taking.

DRESSMAKER'S CARBON

To use dressmaker's carbon, position pattern right side up on fabric, and pin at each corner. Carefully slip carbon paper, carbon side down, between fabric and pattern.

Draw over design lines of pattern, using a tracing wheel. You may find that a knitting needle, used like a pencil, will give you more control when you are drawing over lines.

POUNCING METHODS

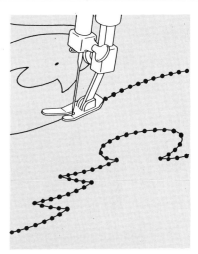

To transfer a design by pouncing method, lay pattern on a thick wad of fabric (an old blanket will do). Using a sharp pin or stiletto prick along design lines of pattern; keep holes close together. **To speed up the work,** use your sewing machine. Remove top and bobbin threads, and set stitch length to large. Stitch along the design lines.

Position design, right side up, on fabric, and pin along all edges. Using a small roll or pad of felt, gently rub pounce (special powder for the purpose) over pricked holes.

Remove pattern carefully to avoid smudging the pounce. Gently blow off excess powder. Use dressmaker's pencil, or a fine brush and water-colour, to connect dots.

15

General embroidery techniques

Using an embroidery hoop

The purpose of an embroidery hoop is to hold the fabric taut during stitching, so that stitch tension can be kept even and consistent. Hoops may be made of wood or plastic, and are available in different widths and diameter sizes ranging from 10 cm to 30 cm. Both wood and plastic hoops usually have a screw on the outer ring for adjusting the fit as necessary.

To secure the fabric in a hoop, follow the instructions below, making certain that fabric grain is running straight in both directions. When you think the fabric is properly secured, tap it lightly; it should feel like a drum. To protect delicate fabrics, or stitches already worked, use either tissue paper or the tape method, shown bottom right. To secure fabric firmly, even if frame is warped, bind both inner and outer rings with tape.

Although there is no set rule as to which part of a design to centre first, always try to get a full motif within the hoop. For example, if your design is of a flower garden, try centring one full flower within the hoop. If the flower is too large, centre only a portion of it, like three complete petals. Small embroidery motifs can be worked in a hoop if backstitched at the edges to pieces of fabric.

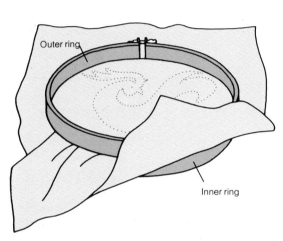

Outer ring

Inner ring

1. With the design side up, place fabric over inner ring of hoop. Adjust screw on outer ring so it fits snugly over inner ring and fabric.

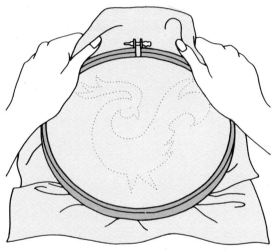

2. Move slowly around the hoop, pushing outer ring down with heels of hands while pulling fabric taut between thumb and fingers.

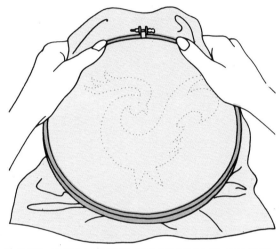

3. Pulling on fabric can make outer ring ride up. To correct this, push outer ring down over inner ring until it is secure.

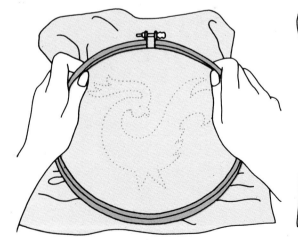

4. Always release fabric from hoop before storing. Press down fabric at edges of hoop with thumbs, lifting outer ring at same time.

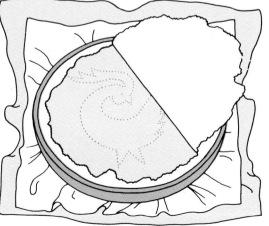

To protect fabric or stitches pressed between rings, place tissue paper over fabric, then fit in hoop. Tear away paper as shown.

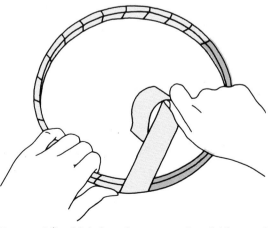

To prevent fine fabric from damage, wrap tape tightly around inner ring as shown; secure ends with masking tape.

Preparing threads

Working threads should be no longer than 50 cm; a longer thread, pulled too often through the fabric, tends to fray and lose its sheen towards the end.

Stranded cotton and Persian wool are both loosely twisted threads that can be separated into finer strands (see below for separating techniques). It is best to separate these threads as you need them rather than all at once.

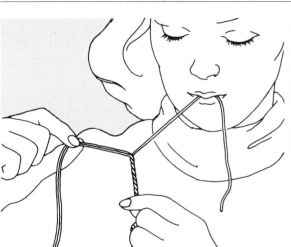

The first step, for either stranded cotton or Persian wool, is to separate from the total strands the number that you want to work with.

To separate stranded cotton, after dividing strands as shown above, hold one group of strands in your mouth, the other in one hand. Hold rest of cotton length with your free hand. Then gently pull the divided strands apart, moving your free hand slowly down the cotton length to control its twisting action.

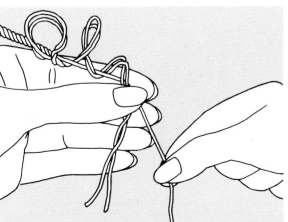

When strands of Persian wool have been undone as in top illustration, lay the wool over your left hand; gently pull out a small quantity of the selected strand with your right hand. Stop, then straighten the remaining strands of wool with left hand to keep them from tangling. Continue pulling and straightening in this way until the entire length is separated.

Threading the needle

There are several ways to simplify needle threading. One is to use a **needle threader,** a handy device specially designed for the purpose. If a threader is not available, try either the **paper strip** or the **looping** method below. Whichever method you choose, be sure that the selected thread can ride easily through the eye of the needle, but not so easily that it will constantly slip out.

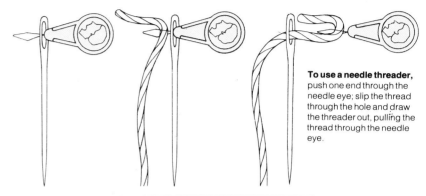

To use a needle threader, push one end through the needle eye; slip the thread through the hole and draw the threader out, pulling the thread through the needle eye.

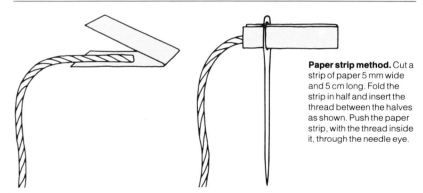

Paper strip method. Cut a strip of paper 5 mm wide and 5 cm long. Fold the strip in half and insert the thread between the halves as shown. Push the paper strip, with the thread inside it, through the needle eye.

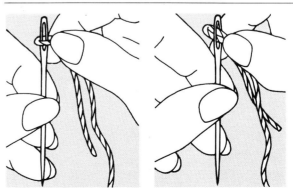

Loop method. Loop end of thread over eye of needle and pull it tight. Slip the loop off the needle and force the fold of the thread through the needle eye.

General embroidery techniques

Working embroidery

Above all else, it takes patience and care to create a successful piece of embroidery. Nothing else will produce the characteristic effects in the stitches that make up the design. You should aim for stitches that are executed at just the right tension, and a finished result that is neat and even on the wrong as well as the right side. The illustrations on the right will help you to reach these goals. Some techniques may seem awkward at first, but they will become easier as practice makes you more proficient.

When you are starting or ending a length of thread, never use a knot; it might show through the finished piece or cause lumps on the right side. This is especially true if your embroidery is to be framed. The adjoining illustrations suggest ways of securing thread at the beginning and end. Do not skimp on thread in either process; the ends can begin to work loose after a few washings.

Whether you use an embroidery hoop or a frame, make the most use you can of both hands as you work. You will find the stabbing motion easier to master when your hoop or frame is on a stand – it frees both hands for the push and pull of the needle action.

Before you start to embroider, study your design carefully and notice which of its parts appear to lie on top of other parts. Work first the parts that lie lowest (furthest down), then work the elements above these so that the two overlap. This will give your piece a realistic effect, and also avoid the possibility of fabric showing between parts.

If you are working on one area of the design and would like to move to another in which the same colour thread is used, it is best to secure the thread at the first point and start again rather than trail the thread over a wide space.

Follow the transferred design lines precisely, remembering that they are guides and are not meant to be seen when the embroidery is completed.

STARTING AND ENDING

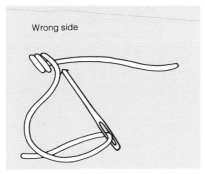

To secure thread at the start of stitching, hold the end of the thread on the wrong side of the fabric and work stitches over 5 cm of thread end.

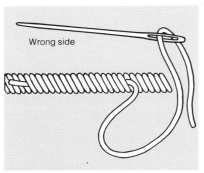

If some embroidery is already worked, simply slide needle under wrong side of laid stitches, securing 5 cm of thread end under the stitching.

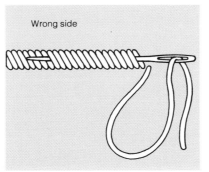

To secure thread at the end of stitching, slide the needle under 5 cm of laid stitches on the wrong side and then cut the thread.

HANDLING NEEDLE

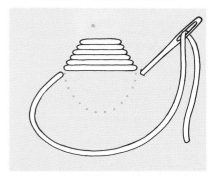

Use stabbing motion whenever possible for an even tension. Push needle straight down and pull thread through, then bring needle straight up.

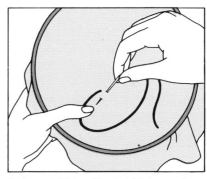

For looped stitches (like chain), bring needle up before thread is pulled through, and use free hand to guide thread around needle.

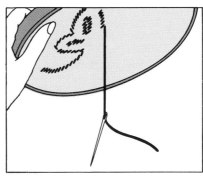

Twisting and tangling often occur with constant needle action. Let needle drop occasionally and dangle freely until thread unwinds.

FOLLOWING DESIGN LINES

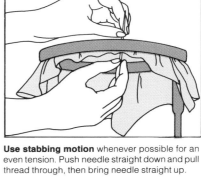

When following design markings on fabric, insert needle on the outside edge of transferred line so that all markings are completely covered.

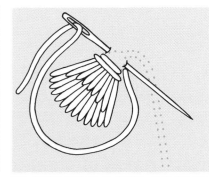

For greater realism in design, work first the parts that lie lowest, then work the parts that lie above them so that the two overlap slightly.

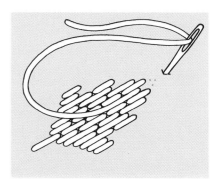

For finer definition of pointed shapes (such as a leaf tip as shown), exaggerate the point by extending the stitch past the transferred line.

Embroidery stitches

Selecting embroidery stitches

Embroidery stitches are the basic components with which a design is carried out. Although the number may seem unlimited, actually each stitch is a part of a stitch family and, as such, has its origin in the basic family stitch. There are 11 such family groups; the pages that follow give step-by-step illustrations for each stitch in each group.

To help you understand the family relationship of one stitch to another, and to provide a means of practicing the stitches, we suggest that you work a sampler of all or some of the stitches you will see on the following pages. You can then keep the sampler as a stitch "dictionary" for future reference or, if you prefer, you can finish it to use as a decorative wall hanging.

Embroidery stitches are used in basically two ways: they either *outline* or *fill* in a particular shape in a design. The shape can be solidly filled so that none of the fabric shows through, or it can be filled with opened stitches for a lacy effect. Some stitches have natural configurations or textures that make them ideal for particular effects. An example is the Vandyke stitch (see p. 36), which gives a natural impression of a leaf when it is worked.

When you make your first attempt at stitch selection, try to limit your choice to a few stitches, and remember that there is no "right" combination of stitches for a design, only one that pleases you and carries out the design to your satisfaction. Notice how the design below has been interpreted in two different ways. Both are lovely pieces, yet each of them was worked with a totally different stitch combination.

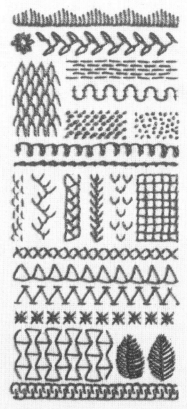

Sampler can serve as a "dictionary" of stitches.

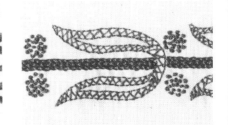

Different stitch interpretations of the identical design can produce two very different impressions.

Charting your design

Prepare a guide for your embroidery work by mapping out a chart that indicates the selected stitches as well as the yarn colours for each part of the design. Use your original traced drawing as the basis for the chart. First assign a *letter* to each stitch and list those stitch symbols at the side. Then print the identifying letters on the appropriate parts of the drawing. Indicate with simple pencil lines the direction in which each stitch will be worked. If colours are not present in your drawing, colour-code the yarns in a similar way: assign a *number* to each coloured yarn and put the numbers on the appropriate parts of the drawing. If there are any other variables, such as the number of yarn strands that are to be used with each stitch, indicate those in your list as well. An example of a charted design is shown below.

A – Long and short stitch   1 – Pale orange
B – Wave stitch   2 – Lavender
C – Basic satin stitch   3 – Black
D – Threaded chain stitch   4 – Tan

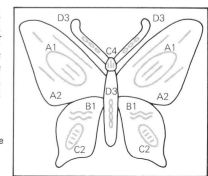

Embroidery stitches

Backstitches

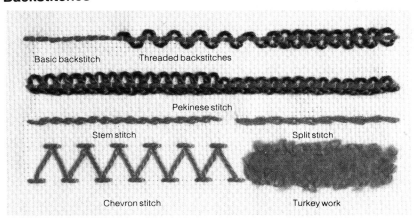

Basic backstitch

Threaded backstitches

Pekinese stitch

Stem stitch

Split stitch

Chevron stitch

Turkey work

Though all of the stitches in the backstitch group have their own distinctive look, they are related in the stitching motion that produces a stitch row. In every case, the needle must be moved a step backwards before a step is taken forwards along the stitch row. This is true whether stitches are being worked from left to right or from right to left.

Some of the stitches shown are narrow, and so are ideal for outlining. In general, *basic backstitch* is used to outline areas bounded by straight lines, and *stem* and *split* stitches are preferred when the boundary line is curved. Worked in close rows, these thin stitches can be used to fill an area. Some of the other stitches, such as *chevron* and *threaded backstitches,* are wider, and therefore suitable for decorative borders and bands. Most of the stitches shown are flat and not highly textured; the exception is *Turkey work,* which creates a soft pile when trimmed.

When working each stitch, be sure to follow carefully the sequence of steps. Because of the backward movement, the needle will often re-enter at a point already established by a previous step; it is important in these instances to insert the needle exactly in the hole that was previously made.

Basic backstitch is most often used as a straight outline stitch. Its simple line effect is often seen in blackwork embroidery. This stitch also forms the base line for other decorative stitches. Work basic stitch from right to left. Bring needle out at 1. Insert at 2 and come up at 3; distance between 3-1 and 1-2 should be equal. Repeat sequence for next stitch; needle entering at point 2 should go into hole made by thread emerging from point 1 of previous stitch. Keep length of backstitches consistent.

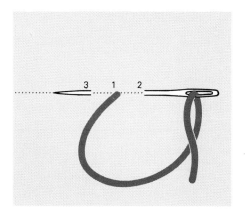
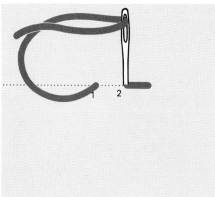
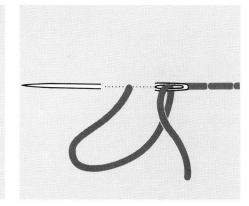

Single or double-threaded backstitches add another dimension to the basic stitch. Worked in contrasting threads, each new row can alter the overall effect. Lay down basic backstitch first. To work *single-threaded* line, use a blunt needle to lace the thread under each stitch; do not catch fabric below. To work *double-threaded* line, lace second thread in opposite direction, keeping loops even on both sides of backstitch line; do not catch or split threads already laid.

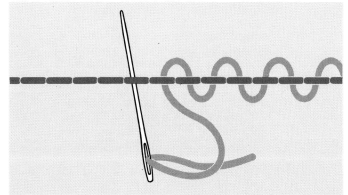
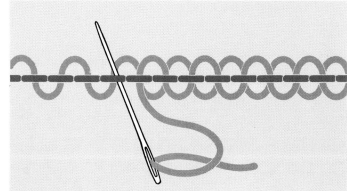

Pekinese stitch (also known as Chinese stitch), like the threaded backstitches, uses simple backstitch as a base. Its interlacing technique, however, produces an effect reminiscent of braid. The stitch is often used for outlining and for decorative borders. Lay down the basic backstitch first. Then, using a blunt needle, lace thread under laid stitches as shown; do not catch fabric below, and keep loops even. Lacing threads can be pulled tighter to eliminate loops above the base line for an even finer braid-like effect.

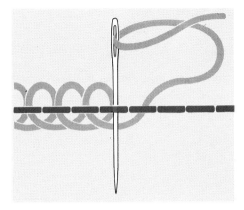 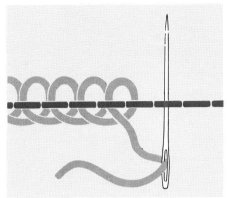 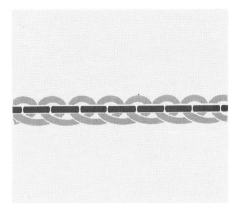

Stem stitch is primarily an outlining stitch, but is often used to work stems. Working from left to right, bring needle out at 1. Insert at 2 and come up a half stitch length back at 3; distance 1-3 and 3-2 should be equal. Repeat sequence. Note that point 3 of previous stitch is now point 1, and the needle emerging at 3 is coming from hole made by thread entering at point 2 of the previous stitch. For a broader stem stitch, angle the needle slightly when entering at 2 and coming up at 3, as shown in the last drawing.

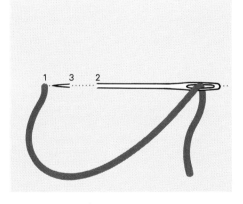 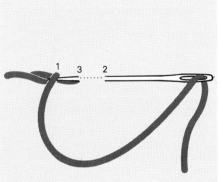 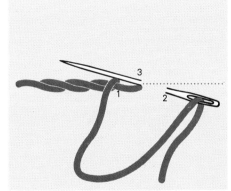

Split stitch is worked like the stem stitch, except when the needle emerges, it splits the working thread. Although outlining is its most common use, split stitch can be used in solid rows as well. Working stitch from left to right, bring needle up at 1 and down at 2. Bring needle back up at 3, splitting centre of laid thread. Repeat sequence. Note that point 3 of previous stitch is now point 1. Keep stitch length even; when going around curves, shorten length slightly. A soft untwisted thread is essential for this stitch.

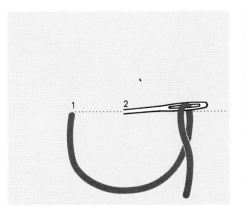 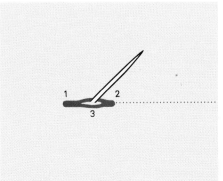 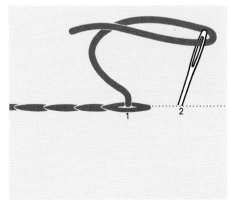

Embroidery stitches

Backstitches

Chevron stitch is often used as a decorative border. The stitch is worked from left to right between double lines. To work stitch, bring needle up at 1 along bottom line. Insert at 2; come up a half stitch length back at 3. Insert needle at point 4 and bring up at 5 along top line; distance between 4-5 is equal to a half stitch length. Bring needle down at 6 (whole stitch length from 5) and back out again at point 4.

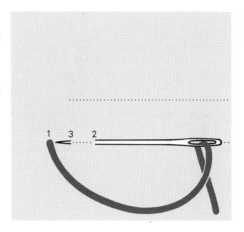
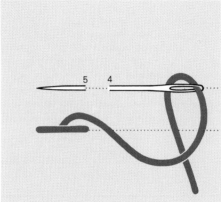
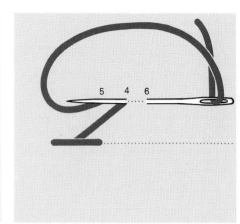

To position needle for repeat, insert needle at 7 on bottom line and come up a half stitch length back at 8; distance between 4-7 is same as 3-4. Continue this 1 to 8 sequence. Note that point 8 is point 1 at start of new sequence.

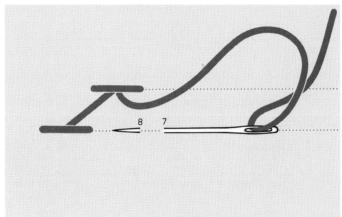
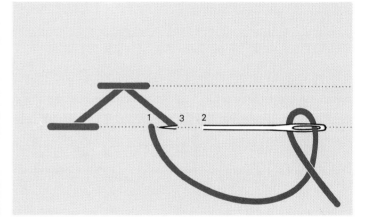

Turkey work is made up of backstitches alternately pulled tight and looped. A series of rows forms a pile, which may be trimmed for a more shaggy effect. Stitch is worked from left to right. Bring the needle out at 1. Insert it at 2 and come up a half stitch length back at 3. Insert the needle at 4, a full stitch length away from 3, and bring it back up at 2; carry thread above stitch line and leave a short loop. Proceed with next backstitch, carrying thread below the stitch line.

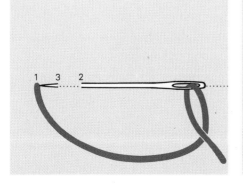
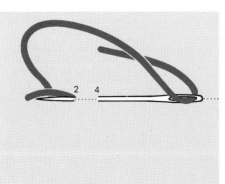
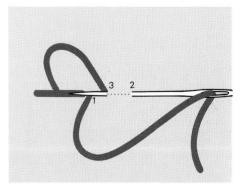

Continue sequence with another looped stitch, then a stitch pulled tight, alternately until row is completed. Cover entire design area with the Turkey work, starting from the top and working towards the bottom. If existing loops get in the way, pin them down. For shaggy pile, cut loops. Do not cut each row individually; instead, trim the entire area at once to a uniform length.

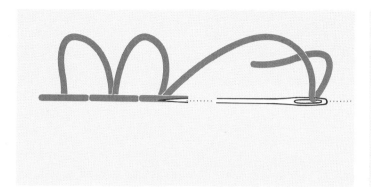

Blanket stitches

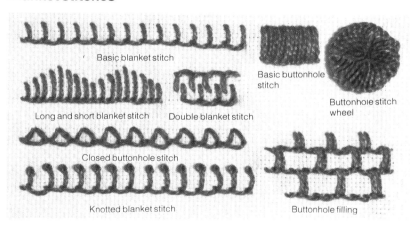

Basic blanket stitch

Long and short blanket stitch   Double blanket stitch

Closed buttonhole stitch

Knotted blanket stitch

Basic buttonhole stitch

Buttonhole stitch wheel

Buttonhole filling

Blanket stitches, which consist basically of edging stitches, comprise the next stitch group. The name probably derived from the finishing worked around the edges of woollen blankets. Today, however, these stitches are often used as outlines and as functional decorative borders as well. One in particular, *buttonhole filling,* can also be worked to cover an entire area, producing an almost crochet-like effect. Blanket stitches are basically flat stitches, neither raised nor textured, and can vary in size depending on the requirements of your design. Because of their adaptability to decorative purposes and the simplicity and speed of working them, they appear in many peasant embroideries, crazy patchwork and appliqué. They are especially useful in hemming embroidery and are also a popular finishing choice for non-woven fabrics, such as felt, that do not require a hem.

You will note that all blanket stitches have a scroll-like base with 'legs' extending from it. This base is formed by looping the thread under the point of the needle before the stitch is pulled up tight. Work carefully to keep stitch height even (unless otherwise specified) and to keep the scroll base at an even tension all the way across.

Basic blanket stitch is a popular finishing stitch for edges. When worked small, it can be used for outlining as well. Stitch is worked from left to right. Bring needle out at 1 on bottom line. Insert at 2 on top line and slightly to the right, then come up at 3, directly below. Before pulling needle through, carry thread under point of needle as shown. Proceed to next stitch. Note point 3 of previous stitch is now point 1. Work entire row in the same way, keeping height of stitches even throughout.

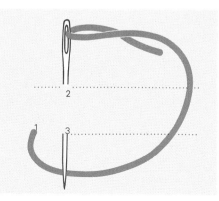
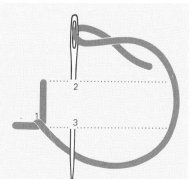
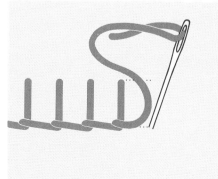

Embroidery stitches

Blanket stitches

Variations of blanket stitch.
The first variation is called *long and short blanket stitch*. It is worked exactly like the basic stitch except that heights of stitches range from short to tall, creating a pyramid effect. *Double blanket stitch* is simply two rows of the basic stitch. Work is turned after one row is completed so that the stitches of the second row can fall between the stitches of the first. Both rows should be the same height and should overlap slightly at the centre.

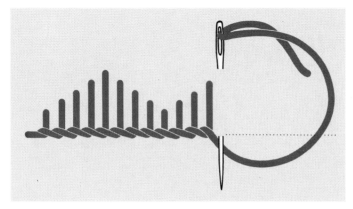
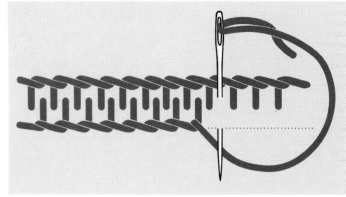

Basic buttonhole stitch is worked like basic blanket stitch, except that the stitches are placed very close together to form a firm edge. This tight little band of stitches is used extensively in cutwork embroidery. For added firmness along an edge, a row of split stitches (p. 21) can be laid along the bottom line first. A *buttonhole stitch wheel* is a popular method for working circular motifs. The basic buttonhole stitch is worked in a circle with the needle entering the same hole in the centre each time.

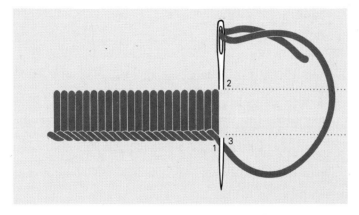
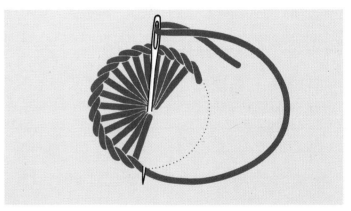

Closed buttonhole stitch is a decorative edging that is worked from left to right. The extending 'legs' form small triangles along the row. Bring needle out at 1 on bottom line. Insert at 2 on top line, slightly to the right, then come up at 3 on bottom line. Before pulling needle through, carry thread under needle point. To complete triangle, insert needle back into 2 again and come out at 4, carrying thread below needle point as usual. Continue sequence as shown. Note that point 4 of the previous stitch is now point 1.

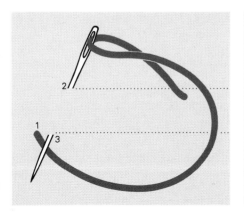
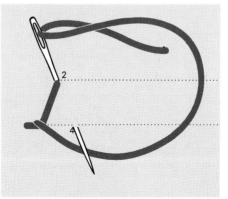
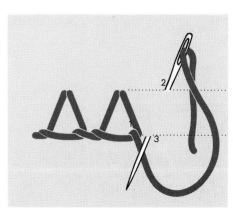

Buttonhole filling consists of several stitched rows that produce a lacy effect. Pairs of buttonhole stitches mesh between other pairs in the row above. (If desired, a group can be three or four stitches.) The buttonhole filling is first worked from left to right, then right to left on the next row. Work the first pair of stitches close together; start the second pair two spaces (width of two stitches) to the right. Continue this way to end of row. Insert needle at end of bottom line, then bring it out at next line directly below to start next row.

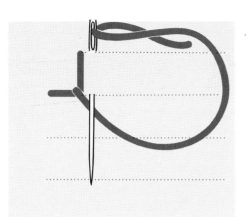 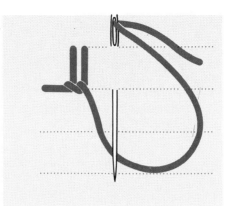 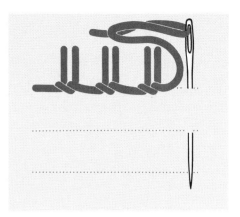

Work the next row from right to left. The basic 1 to 3 buttonhole stitch sequence is still used, but now the thread is carried under the needle point from right to left as shown. Work the pairs of buttonhole stitches over the open spaces on the row above. At end of second row, insert needle in bottom line, then out at next line directly below. Continue working rows in this way until desired area is covered.

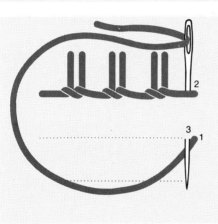 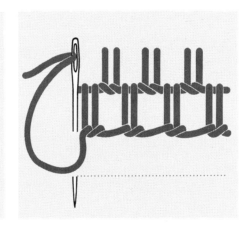 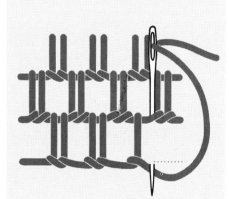

Knotted blanket stitch resembles basic blanket stitch, but with a knot formed at the top of each 'leg'. Working from left to right, bring needle out at 1. Wrap thread around left thumb and place needle point under loop. Slip loop off thumb. With needle inside loop, insert needle at 2 and come up at 3; carry thread under needle point, then pull thread end to tighten loop around needle. Pull needle through to form knot at top of stitch. Continue along entire row. Worked back to back, this stitch makes an attractive tree design (see far right).

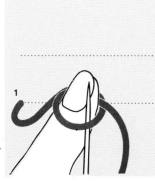 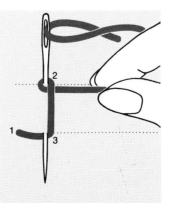 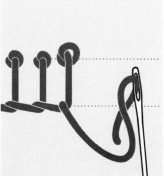 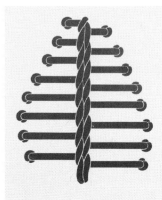

Embroidery stitches

Chain stitches

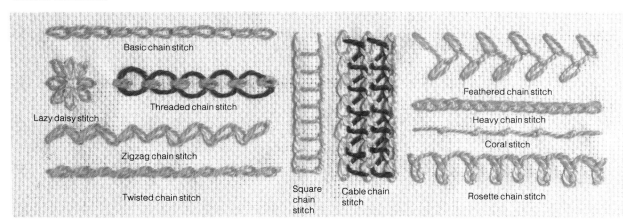

Basic chain stitch

Lazy daisy stitch

Threaded chain stitch

Zigzag chain stitch

Twisted chain stitch

Square chain stitch

Cable chain stitch

Feathered chain stitch

Heavy chain stitch

Coral stitch

Rosette chain stitch

Most of the stitches in this group resemble links in a chain. Each stitch has its own special shape and particular use, but together they form one of the most indispensable of the stitch groups. Chain stitches, like the blanket stitch group, are looped. The working thread is always carried under the needle point before the stitch is pulled tight.

For the most part, these stitches are worked vertically and are used basically for outlining and for decorative borders. If worked in rows to fill an area, all rows are usually stitched in the same direction to give a fabric-like texture. Chain stitch is worked more easily out of a frame.

Basic chain stitch is one of the most popular embroidery stitches for outlining or, if worked in close rows, for filling an area. Bring needle out at 1. Insert back into same hole at point 1 and bring out at 2, carrying thread under needle point, then pull it through. Point 2 is now point 1 of next stitch. Work all stitches the same way, always inserting needle into the hole made by the emerging thread. To end row, take a small stitch over last chain loop to hold it down.

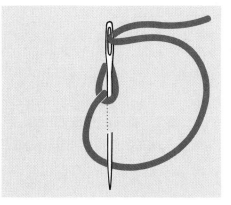

Lazy daisy stitch (or detached chain) is a single unattached stitch, often worked in a circle to give an impression of petals. Bring needle out at 1. Insert back into same hole at point 1, and come up at 2; carry thread under needle point, then pull through. Insert needle at 3 over chain loop, then bring needle out at point 1 for next chain stitch. Continue this way until all petals are completed. Stitches may be scattered at random over an area, provided thread does not have to be carried too far on wrong side.

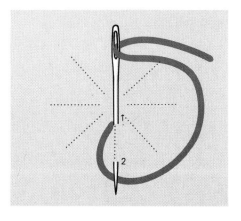

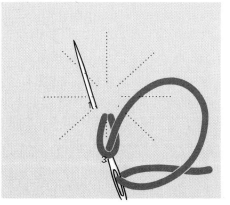

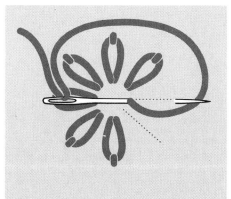

Threaded chain stitch
resembles a chain with two link sizes. To achieve this double link effect, detached chain stitches are threaded with a contrasting thread. This makes a pretty border or outline stitch. First work a row of detached chain stitches. Using a blunt needle and contrasting thread, bring needle up under last chain. Lace thread back and forth under each chain; do not catch fabric. Start again at bottom and lace in opposite direction, keeping loops even on both sides of the detached chain stitches.

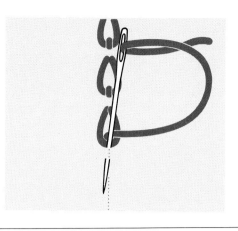
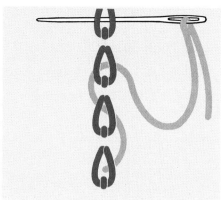
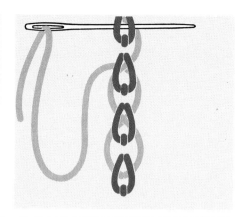

Zigzag chain stitch is worked with the chains positioned at alternating angles to give a decorative zigzag effect. Work first stitch exactly like a basic chain stitch, angling it as shown between double lines. The hole from which thread emerges becomes point 1 for next stitch. Insert needle at 2, piercing loop end to anchor it, and come up at 3; carry thread under needle point, then pull through. Continue sequence, always piercing loop end and keeping angle of stitches consistent. To end, take small stitch over last chain loop.

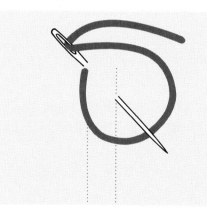
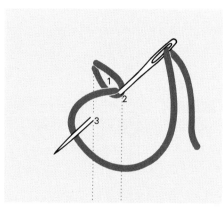

Twisted chain stitch makes an unusual textured outline. To work, bring needle out at 1. Insert needle at 2, which is slightly lower and to the left of 1, then come up at 3, which is in line with 1; carry thread under point of needle, then pull through. Work next stitch the same way. Note that point 3 of previous stitch is point 1 of new stitch. Complete row of chains. To end, take a small stitch over the last chain loop to hold it down.

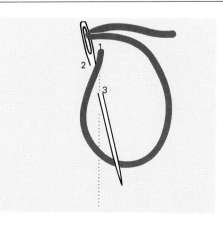
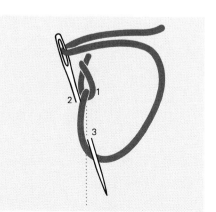
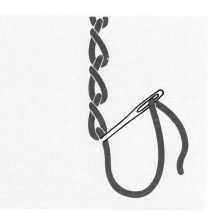

Embroidery stitches

Chain stitches

Square chain stitch (or ladder stitch) provides broad outline that may be laced with ribbon or thread. Stitch is worked between double lines. Bring needle out at 1 on left line. Insert at 2, directly across, and come up at 3; carry thread under needle point, then pull through. Do not pull thread tight; leave some slack so that needle can be inserted inside wide loop for next stitch. Continue this way until row is completed. To anchor last chain, take a small stitch over left side of loop, then take a small stitch over right side.

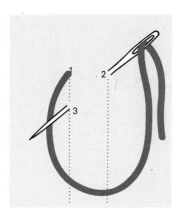 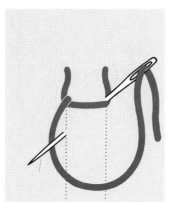 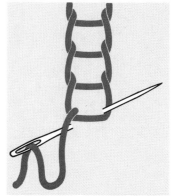 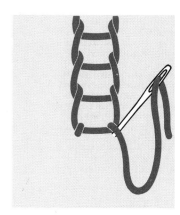

Cable chain stitch resembles a metal chain. It can be used for outlining or interlaced for a filling as in the last illustration. Bring needle out at 1. Loop thread over needle as shown. Insert needle at 2, just below point 1, and come up at 3; carry thread under needle point. As you pull needle through, both small and large links are formed. Continue this way until the row is completed. To interlace, work several rows of cable chain stitch, then use a blunt needle with contrasting thread to weave in and out.

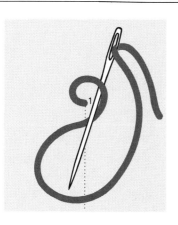 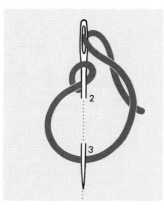 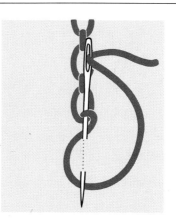 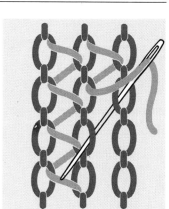

Feathered chain stitch is a delicate border stitch that resembles a vine. It is worked between double lines. Starting at one side of double line, work a slanted chain stitch in the basic 1 to 2 sequence shown. Insert needle at 3, then bring it back up at 4, approximately across from 2. Work subsequent chain stitches the same way, keeping alternating slants of chains consistent on each side.

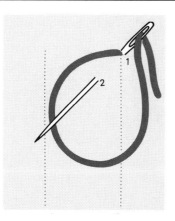 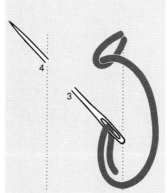 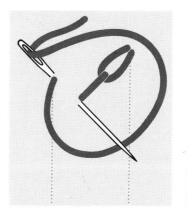 

Heavy chain stitch makes a pretty outline stitch. Because of its plait-like quality, it can also be used for stems, twigs and narrow leaves. To start, work a basic chain stitch by bringing needle out at 1, then inserting needle back in same hole and coming up at 2. Insert needle down at 3 over chain loop, then come back up at 4, which is same distance from 2 as 1 is from 2. Slide needle under first chain stitch from right to left without picking up any fabric. Re-insert needle at 4, and come up at 5.

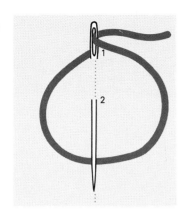 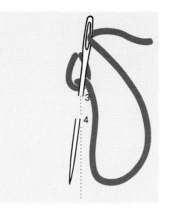 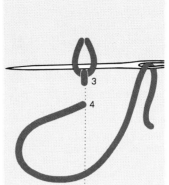 

Slide needle from right to left under the second chain stitch and the small anchoring stitch, then re-insert needle at 5, and bring out at 6. Slide needle from right to left under the two preceding chain stitches as shown, then re-insert needle at 6. Continue in this way, always sliding needle under the last two chain stitches.

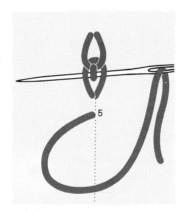 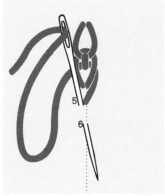 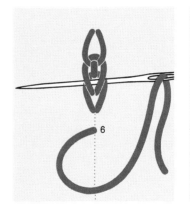 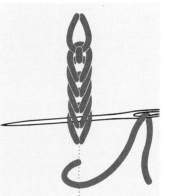

Coral stitch is a simple outline stitch, punctuated with small knots along the row. It is particularly effective used for stems and twigs. If worked in many rows, coral stitch can also fill an area with an unusual texture. Work stitch from right to left. Bring needle up at 1. Insert needle at 2, then take a small bite of fabric slanting needle out at 3. Loop thread over and around needle point, then pull needle through to secure stitch and form knot. Continue in this way for entire row, spacing knots evenly or at random as you wish.

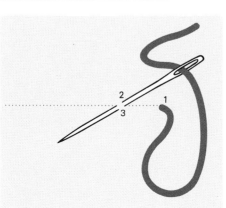 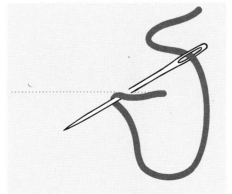 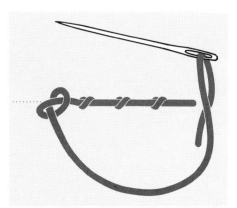

Embroidery stitches

Chain stitches

Rosette chain stitch, a neat edging, is worked small and close together. Work stitch from right to left between double lines. Bring needle out at 1. To make rosette, insert at 2, slightly to the left, then out at 3 directly below; carry thread under needle and pull through. Slide needle under thread at 1; leave a little slack along top. Work next stitch a short distance away, entering at 2 and coming up at 3; slide needle under slack thread at top. To end row, insert needle back into point 2 of last rosette.

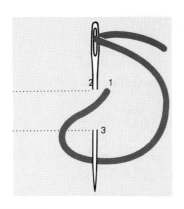
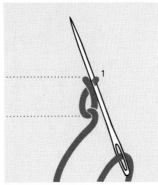
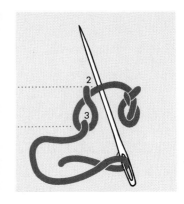
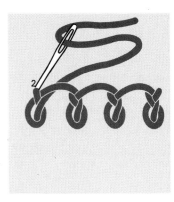

Couching

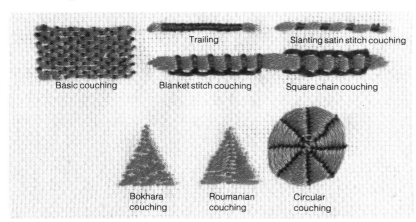

Basic couching

Trailing

Slanting satin stitch couching

Blanket stitch couching

Square chain couching

Bokhara couching

Roumanian couching

Circular couching

This group of stitches, known as couching stitches, is particularly useful in outlining an area or in giving more weight to a single line. Usually, there are two working threads, the laid thread (which can be one or more strands) and the couching thread. The couching thread is stitched over the laid thread to attach it to the fabric. Often the laid thread and the couching thread are of contrasting colours. The actual effect of couching varies with the specific stitch and the number of laid threads that are used.

The more strands you lay down, the heavier the outline. Experiment to determine how many strands should be laid. You will need more strands to outline a heavily embroidered shape than to define a delicate pattern.

In addition to outlining, whole areas can be filled in with couching. This is known as laid work. To create textural variety, lay the threads so that they run in different directions.

Two unusual types of couching are *Bokhara* and *Roumanian.* Both employ only one length of thread for both the laying and the couching.

To create more unusual effects, couch over finished canvas work and appliqué. Or try couching with suitable metallic threads.

Basic couching is used to outline a design. To start, bring up desired number of laid threads on right. Use left thumb to hold and guide laid threads as you couch over them. Bring working thread up at 1 just below laid threads. Insert at 2 directly above laid threads, and come up at 3 further along the line. Point 3 is now point 1 for next stitch. Continue until laid threads are completely anchored; keep distance between stitches consistent. Take ends of laid threads to back of work and secure.

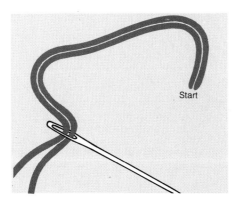
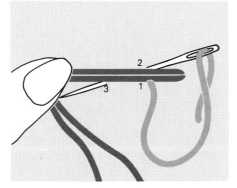
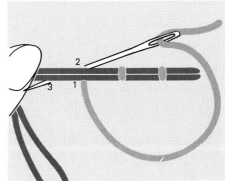

Start

To fill an area, work first line as in basic couching. At end of line, turn trailing laid threads to the right. Take a horizontal stitch at turning point. Turn work *upside-down* and couch second row of threads from right to left, placing stitches between stitches of preceding row. At end of second row, turn trailing laid threads to the right and again take a horizontal stitch. Turn work *upright* and work third row, alternating vertical stitches with those in the row above. Continue this way until entire area is covered.

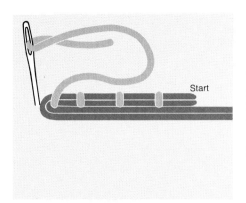

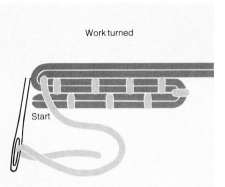

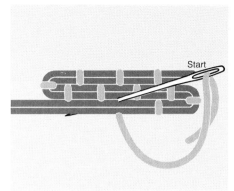

Work turned

Start

Start

Start

Variations can be achieved by working some basic embroidery stitches over the laid threads. Four are shown on the right. The first is similar to basic couching except that *straight satin stitches* are worked close together to completely cover the laid threads; this produces a raised, textured line known as trailing. The next is couched with pairs of *slanting satin stitches*. The third and fourth types are couched with *blanket stitches* and *square chain stitches*, respectively, over several laid threads.

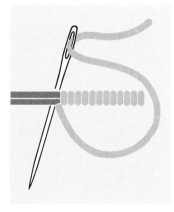

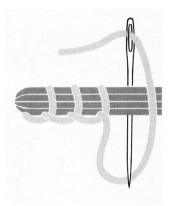

Bokhara couching is used to fill an area with a woven effect. Unlike the previous couching, both the laid and the couching threads are one and the same. The thread is laid from left to right and couched from right to left. Bring thread up at 1. Insert at 2, and come up at 3 above laid thread. Insert needle at 4 over laid thread and slightly to the left of 3. Come up at 5 (in line with 3). Continue slanted stitches to end of laid thread. Bring needle out at 1 to begin next row. Place slanted stitches in each row between those in previous row.

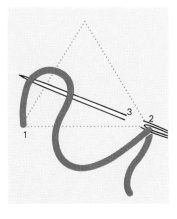

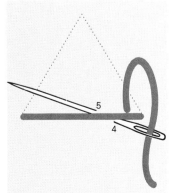

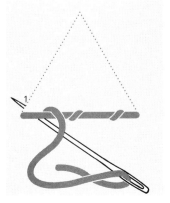

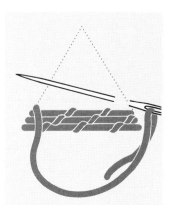

Embroidery stitches

Couching

Roumanian couching, like Bokhara, uses same thread length for laid and couching threads. The two stitches are worked similarly, but the Roumanian stitches are longer. Bring thread up at 1. Insert at 2, come up at 3 above laid thread. Take a long slanting stitch over laid thread to 4; come up at 1 for start of next row. Continue taking laid and couching stitches, keeping threads slack so that the two stitch types appear indistinguishable. Place each new slanting stitch above one in previous row.

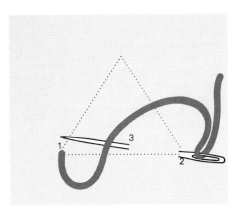 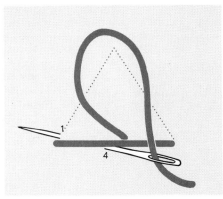 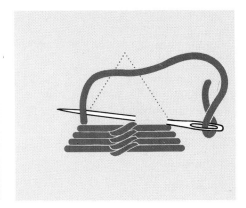

Circular couching produces a solid spoked-wheel effect. It is particularly effective in contrasting threads. Bring couching thread up at 1 in centre of marked circle. Loop laid thread over couching thread as shown, and re-insert needle at 1 to secure laid thread. Bring needle out at 2 along one of the spoke lines, then take a small stitch over the laid threads by inserting needle at 3 directly above 2. Bring needle out at 4 along next spoke line. Take another stitch at 5 over laid threads.

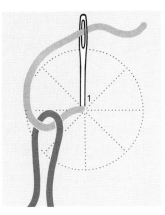 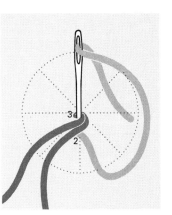 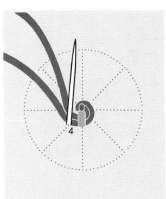 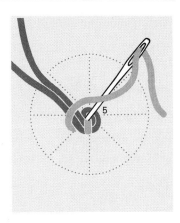

Continue taking small stitches over laid threads at each marked spoke line while guiding the laid threads around centre in a clockwise direction. Be careful not to pull laid threads too tightly or work will pucker. When circle is completed, fasten off couching thread on wrong side. Thread one of the laid threads; take to back of fabric and secure. Thread second laid thread and wind around circle past end of first laid thread (to make circle end gradually). Take to back and secure as before.

 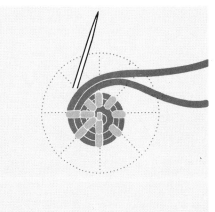 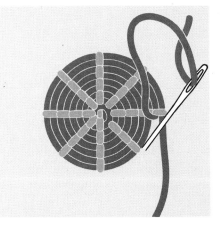 

Cross stitches

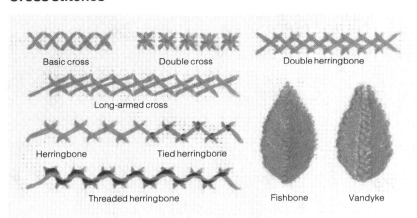

Basic cross

Double cross

Double herringbone

Long-armed cross

Herringbone

Tied herringbone

Threaded herringbone

Fishbone

Vandyke

Cross stitches make up the next group of embroidery stitches. As their name implies, all the stitches in this category are formed in one way or another by two crossing arms. The uses of cross stitches are numerous; they can be worked as outlines, as borders, or to fill in an entire area. Sometimes crossing stitches overlap, as in *herringbone stitches*. Two such overlapping stitches, *fishbone stitch* and *Vandyke stitch*, are particularly well suited to the formation of leaves.

The basic cross stitch is, of course, the best known stitch and in itself qualifies as an embroidery technique. Its even stitch formation makes it ideal for working on even-weave and printed fabrics, such as gingham (see p. 66). Unlike cross stitch variations, basic cross stitches (when worked in a row) can be stitched in two journeys. Half of the stitch is laid on one journey, then the crossing arm is laid on the return. This stitching technique helps to ensure an even stitch tension. For a good appearance, make sure that all of the top threads lie in the same direction.

The basic cross stitch can be used to create an intaglio effect. This is a very useful technique that involves covering the background, leaving the design free of stitching.

Basic cross stitch's simplicity and versatility make it a highly popular stitch. Cross stitches are usually *worked in rows* of even, slanted stitches, first from right to left laying down half the crosses, then back from left to right to complete them. Bring needle up at 1. Insert at 2 and come up at 3 directly below 2. At end of row, work back, entering at 4 and coming up at 5. To *work one cross stitch* at a time, bring needle up at 1. Insert at 2 and come up at 3 directly below 2. Insert needle at 4, above 1.

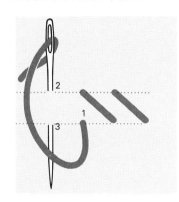

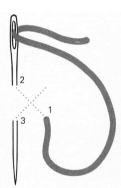

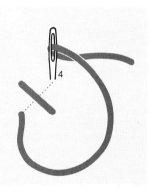

Double cross stitch resembles a star and can be scattered as a filling stitch or worked in a row to provide a decorative border. It is worked very similarly to the basic single cross stitch above. Bring needle out at 1. Insert at 2 and come up at 3 directly below 2. Enter at 4 and come up at 5 (halfway between points 1 and 3). Insert at 6 directly above 5 (halfway between points 2 and 4) and come up at 7 (halfway between 2 and 3). Insert at 8 directly across from 7 to complete stitch.

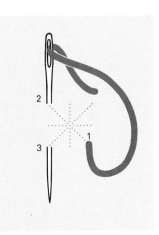

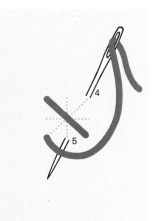

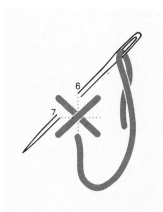

Embroidery stitches

Cross stitches

Long-armed cross stitch gives an almost plaited effect as each cross stitch overlaps the next. The first arm of the cross is longer and has a more extreme slant than the second. Work stitch from left to right. Bring needle up at 1. Take a long slanting stitch to top right, inserting needle at 2; come up half a step back at 3. Insert needle at 4 directly below point 2; then bring needle up at 1 directly below point 3, for start of next stitch. Repeat sequence. Note that each stitch touches the previous one at the top and overlaps it at the bottom.

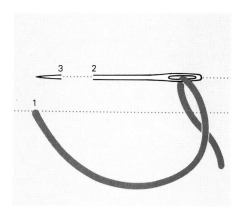 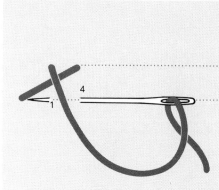 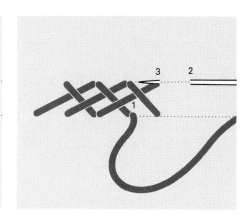

Herringbone stitch is a popular embroidery stitch often used for borders. This basic overlapping stitch forms a foundation that can be decorated with a second colour. Keep the spacing and length of stitches even. Work from left to right. Bring needle up at 1. Take a slanting stitch to the top right, inserting needle at 2. Come up a short distance back at 3; insert needle at 4 to complete stitch. Bring needle up at 1 to start new stitch. Repeat sequence for each subsequent stitch.

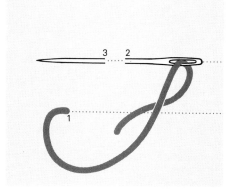 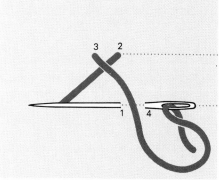 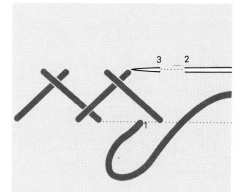

Tied herringbone stitch adds another dimension to the basic herringbone stitch above; each cross of the stitch is tied down with a small vertical stitch of a contrasting colour thread. Work a row of herringbone stitch first, using the 1 to 4 sequence above. To tie down crosses, work from right to left. Bring needle out at A just above top, right-hand cross. Insert at B and come up at C below next cross. Insert needle at D; come up at point A for the start of a new sequence. Continue in this way until all crosses are tied down.

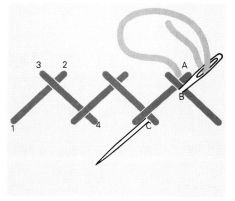 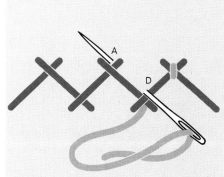 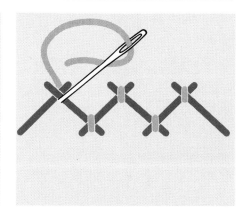

Threaded herringbone stitch
is another variation of the basic herringbone stitch. Here, a contrasting colour thread is laced over and under the crosses. The needle does not pierce the fabric, so use a blunt needle for the lacing. Start lacing from the left side so that the needle passes under each arm of the cross and over the intersecting points as shown. Do not pull lacing too tightly or you will distort the basic herringbone stitch.

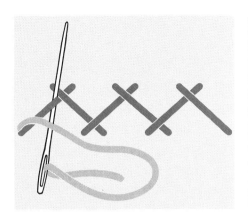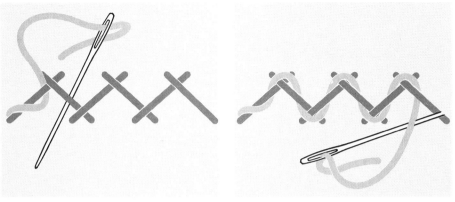

Double herringbone stitch is two rows of herringbone stitches that interlace. Rows worked in contrasting colours are especially attractive. For interlaced look, each row is worked slightly differently from herringbone stitch. Work both rows from left to right. Bring needle up at 1. Take a slanting stitch to top right, inserting needle at 2. Come up a short distance back at 3. Slip needle *under first slanting arm.* Insert at 4 to complete stitch. Repeat sequence, always slipping needle under first slanting arm of each cross.

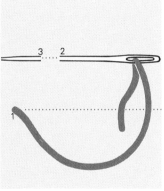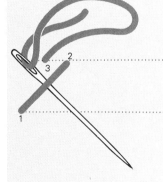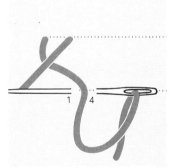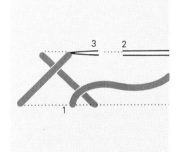

Change to contrasting thread. To get into position for second herringbone sequence, come out at A directly above point 1, and insert at B directly below point 2, crossing over arm 1-2 in original colour. Bring needle out at C directly below point 3, and pass needle under arm 3-4 (original colour). Insert needle at D and come up at E. Pass needle under arm C-D; insert at F. To complete sequence, bring needle out at C for start of next repeat. Continue, repeating sequence C to F, passing each time over and under appropriate slanting arms.

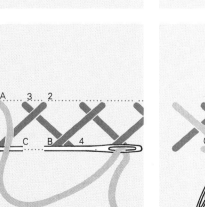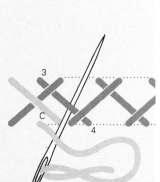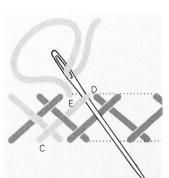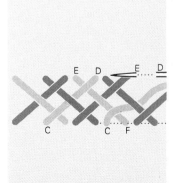

Embroidery stitches

Cross stitches

Fishbone stitch is a type of cross stitch used primarily for leaf designs. The crosses are not immediately evident because the crossing points occur at the base of the arms. To establish tip of leaf, bring needle up at 1 and take a short stitch down centre to 2. Bring needle up at 3 close to first stitch; insert at 4 just to right of middle line. Emerge at 5 directly across from 3. Insert needle at 6 just to left of centre line. Repeat the 3 to 6 sequence by bringing needle up at the new point 3. Continue this sequence until leaf shape is completely filled.

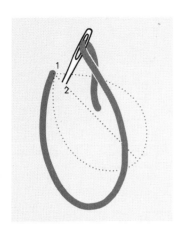
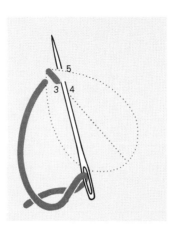
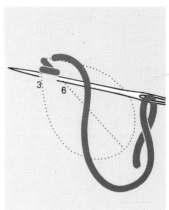

Vandyke stitch is another variation of cross stitch used for leaf designs. As the stitch is worked, a thin plaited line is formed in the centre to represent the centre vein of the leaf. The first four steps in the following series start the design; the fifth and sixth steps are repeated in sequence thereafter. Bring needle out at 1 on left side below tip. Insert at 2 and come up at 3 taking a small bite at leaf tip. Insert needle at 4 directly across from 1. Bring needle out at 5 on left side. Pass needle *under the pair of crossed threads* above.

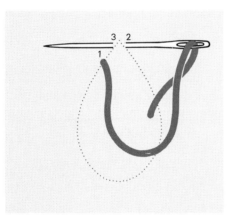
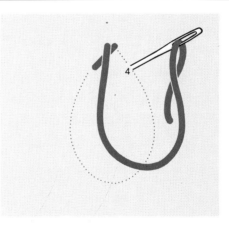
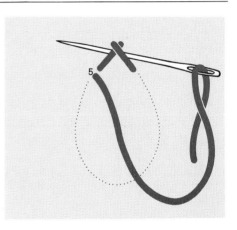

Insert needle at 6 on the right side and bring needle out at left side again for next stitch. Continue 5 to 6 sequence until leaf design is filled, always passing needle under last two crossed threads. Worked between narrow parallel lines, stitch forms a fine raised plait for a decorative outline or border. When worked in adjacent rows, it produces a pebbly texture. Squares or rectangles of this stitch worked at right-angles can convey the texture of bricks or paving stones.

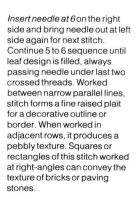
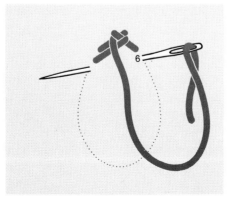

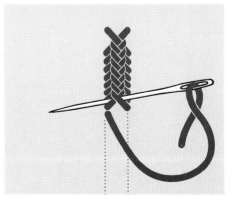

Feather stitches

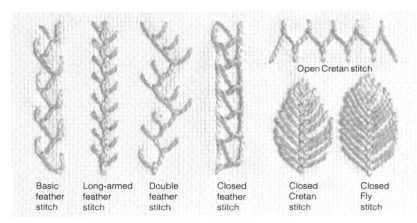

Basic feather stitch   Long-armed feather stitch   Double feather stitch   Closed feather stitch   Closed Cretan stitch   Closed Fly stitch

Open Cretan stitch

The feather stitches make up the next category of embroidery stitches. Originally used to decorate 19th-century English smocks, most of the feather stitches are used today for borders on edges and hems. Their feather-like look comes from their being open looped stitches taken alternately to the right and the left from a central core.

Two of the feather stitch variations, *closed Cretan* and *Fly stitches*, are often used for filling leaf and fern designs. When worked, they both have a textured centre that resembles the main vein of a leaf.

The basic feather stitch and its varia-

tions are often seen in crazy patchwork (stitched over the adjoining edges of patches) and in appliqué. They are also used to add a delicate edge to children's and babies' clothes.

Like the earlier blanket and chain stitches, feather stitches are looped; the working thread must be carried under the point of the needle before it is pulled tight. Because of the back-and-forth movement of the needle, care must be taken to keep the stitches even on both sides of the centre line. Before stitching, it is useful to lightly draw guidelines for the centre line as well as the side lines of leaf edges.

Basic feather stitch is a looped stitch that is evenly worked with stitches alternating to the left and to the right. Work stitches from top to bottom. Bring needle up at 1 in centre. Insert needle at 2 slightly lower and to the right. Then angle needle out at 3 along centre line, carrying working thread under point; pull through. Insert needle at 4 slightly below and to left of 3. Angle needle out at 5 along centre line; carry thread under point and pull through. Continue, alternating angle of looped stitches. To end row, take a small stitch over last loop.

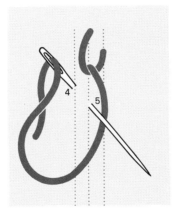

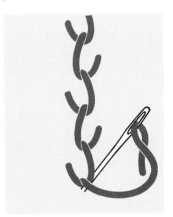

Long-armed feather stitch (or Cretan stitch) is worked like the basic stitch except that the longer half of each loop is on the outside. Bring needle up at 1 in centre. Insert needle at 2 slightly higher and to the right, then angle needle out at 3 along centre line. Carry thread under needle; pull through. Insert needle at 4 slightly higher and to left of 3 (distance between 1-2 and 3-4 should be equal), then angle needle out at 5 along centre. Carry thread under needle and pull through. Repeat 1-5 to end.

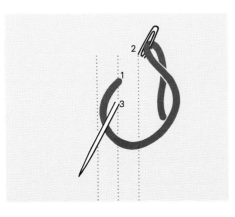
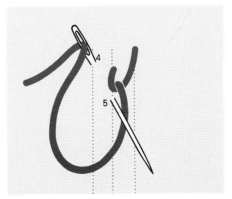
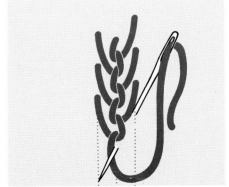

Embroidery stitches

Feather stitches

Double feather stitch makes an airy, zigzag border. Instead of a single looped stitch placed alternately left and right, two stitches are made consecutively to one side and then to the other. Keep the loops even. To start, bring needle up at 1 in centre. Insert at 2 directly across. Angle needle left and out at 3; carry thread under point of needle and pull. Insert at 4 directly across from 3. Angle right, coming out at 5; carry thread under needle and pull. Insert needle at 6. Angle right, coming out at 7; carry thread under needle and pull.

To complete sequence, insert needle at 8 directly across from 7 and below 3. Angle left and out at 9; carry thread under needle point and pull. Two sets of looped stitches are now complete. Repeat sequence from start. Note that point 9 of last sequence is point 1 of the new sequence. Continue with 1 to 9 series until row is completed.

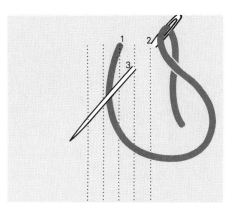
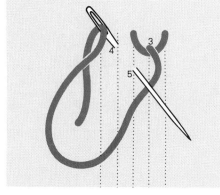
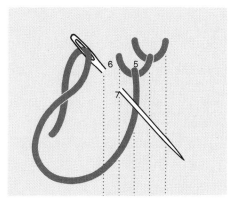

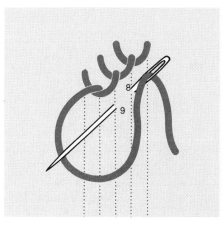
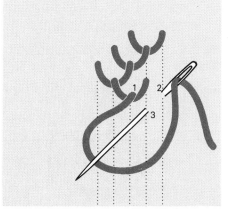
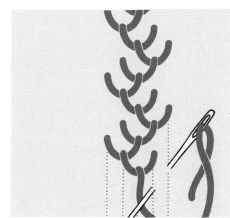

Closed feather stitch is a simple variation of the basic stitch in which each stitch *touches the previous one,* leaving no space between. To achieve this, the stitches are made *vertically* rather than at an angle. Bring needle up at 1. Insert at 2, half a step up and to the right of 1; emerge at 3 a full step below. Carry thread under needle point and pull through. Insert needle at point 4 just below 1, so that the threads touch. Emerge a full step below at 5. Repeat sequence, always inserting needle just below previous stitch to form an unbroken line.

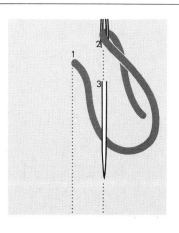
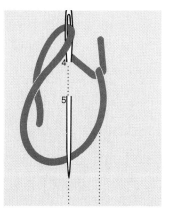
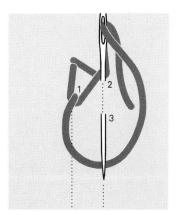
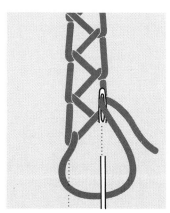

Open Cretan stitch is a type of feather stitch that produces a decorative border. Unlike most feather stitches, it is worked horizontally. Bring needle up at 1. Insert at 2 above and to right; come up at 3 directly below 2. Carry thread under point and pull through. Insert needle at 4 on bottom and further to the right; come up at 5 directly above 4. Carry thread under point and pull through. Continue in this way, always placing each stitch to the right of the last one and keeping the distance between stitches even.

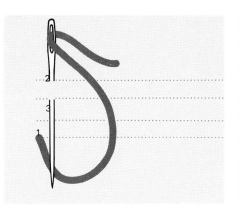
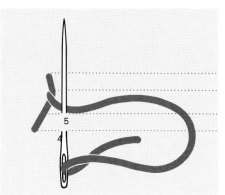
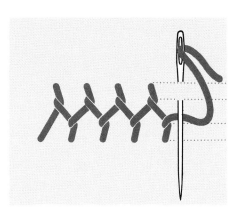

Closed Cretan stitch is usually used as a leaf-filling stitch as it forms a natural plait down the centre. Bring needle up at leaf top, 1. Insert at 2 and come up at 3, slightly to the right of the centre line. Carry thread under needle point and pull through. Insert needle at 4 directly across from 2; come up at 5 directly across from 3 and slightly to the left of centre. Carry thread under needle and pull. Start next stitch on right side, then alternate, bringing needle out either to the left or to the right of the centre line to create centre plait.

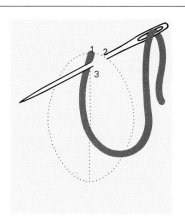
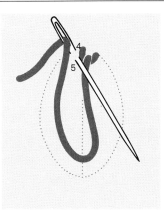

Closed Fly stitch is another leaf-filling stitch. It has a spine down the centre. Bring needle up at 1 and take a small stitch down centre to 2. Bring needle up at 3; insert at 4 directly across from 3. Come up at hole originally made at 2; carry thread under needle point and pull through. Proceed to next stitch. Note that point 2 of previous stitch (where thread emerges) is point 1 of next stitch. Continue this way until leaf design is filled.

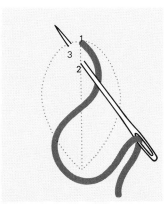
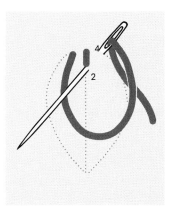
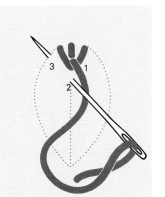

Embroidery stitches

Filling stitches/detached

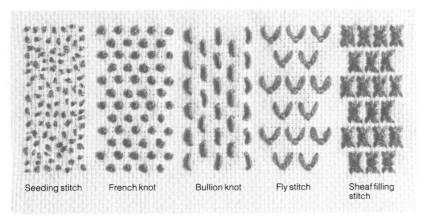

Seeding stitch   French knot   Bullion knot   Fly stitch   Sheaf filling stitch

Although all the stitches in this next set are quite different from one another, each having its own unique look, they have one thing in common – they are all detached, single stitches used primarily as a means of filling in a design area. All the stitches presented here contribute great textural variation to an embroidered piece. Certain especially raised stitches, among them the *French knot* and the *bullion knot,* can be flattened by an embroidery hoop. When using a hoop, take care to avoid crushing raised stitches (see p. 16).

Because each of these stitches has such an individual look, it can serve many purposes besides filling. The French knot is a particular favourite of embroiderers. It can be used singly to represent a feature such as an eye, or a number of knots can be grouped to form a texture. Another versatile stitch is *seeding stitch,* which can be scattered lightly or heavily to give a shaded effect. *Fly stitch* and *sheaf filling stitch* both require a little more planning in the placing. Worked in rows, they can be used as a border. They can also be worked singly. Scattered fly stitches resemble distant birds in flight; sheaf filling stitches look very much like bundles of wheat.

Seeding stitch is one of the simplest filling stitches. It can be used in clusters or scattered. If worked close together, groups of seeding stitches can even be a means of shading. Bring needle up at 1 and take a tiny stitch down at 2. For a heavier stitch, bring needle up at 3 and take another small stitch at 4 close to the first stitch. Scatter seeding stitches as desired, changing the direction of the stitches for a varied effect. If all stitches are worked in one direction, filling will be uniform.

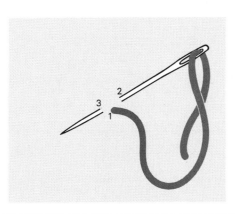

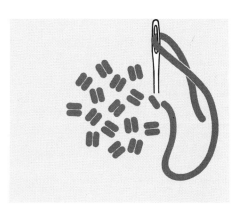

The French knot is used like the seeding stitch, but it is considerably more textured and raised. Knots can be worked close together to fill an area completely, producing a knobbly effect. Bring needle up at 1. Holding thread taut with left hand, wrap thread around needle twice as shown; gently pull the thread so the twists are tightened against the needle. Carefully insert needle near point 1 and pull through; be sure thread end is still held taut. Scatter knots as desired within design area. French knots can be made larger by using a thicker thread.

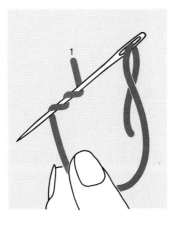
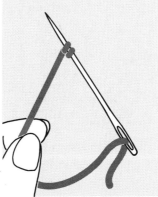
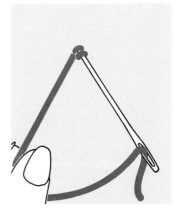

40

Bullion knot can be used as a filling or as an outline stitch. Bring needle up at 1. Insert at 2 and come up at 1 again, but leave needle in fabric. Twist thread around needle point five to seven times depending on length of stitch (distance from 1 to 2). Then carefully pull needle through both fabric and twists; take care not to distort twists. Pull thread towards point 2 so that coil can lie flat. Pull working thread tight and use point of needle to pack threads in coil together evenly. Re-insert needle into point 2.

 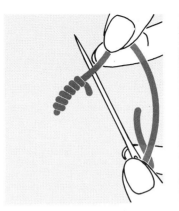 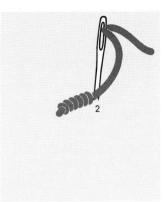

Fly stitch is a single, looped stitch not unlike the basic feather stitch. When completed it resembles a Y. It can be scattered about as a filling, lined up for a border, or used as a leaf filling (p. 39). Bring needle up at 1. Insert at 2 directly across, then angle needle out at 3. Points 1, 2 and 3 should be equidistant. Carry the thread under the needle point and pull through. Complete stitch by inserting at 4 over loop. Work as many fly stitches as necessary to fill design area.

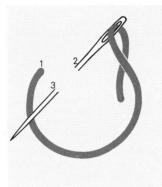 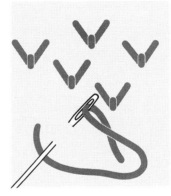 

Sheaf filling stitch resembles a tied bundle of wheat. Stitches can be arranged in alternate rows or set close together, one right below another. Bring needle out at 1. Work three satin stitches, following numbered sequence shown. Bring needle up at point 7, midway between 5 and 6. Pass needle around the stitch bundles twice without piercing fabric and pull thread taut. Insert needle under bundle and through fabric; secure stitch on back of work. For a different effect, work the tying stitches in a contrasting thread colour.

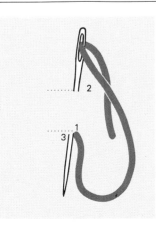 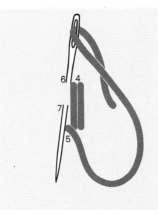 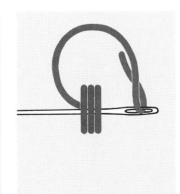 

41

Embroidery stitches

Filling stitches/laid work

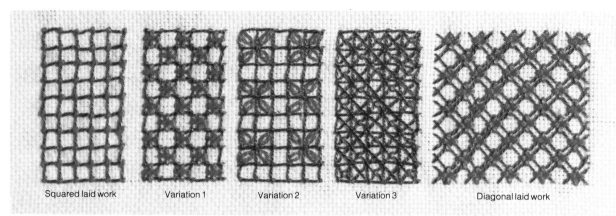

Squared laid work   Variation 1   Variation 2   Variation 3   Diagonal laid work

A fairly large design area can be attractively filled with this next group of embroidered filling stitches. These stitches are longer than the preceding detached ones and are laid to create the effect of a grid or lattice. The basic lattice is laid down, then anchored down at its intersections to keep them in place.

Embellishments can then be added: this is usually done with contrasting thread. In laying down the long, grid-like stitches, take care to ensure even and consistent spacing. Do not pull thread too tight as work will pucker.

It is essential for laid work that the fabric be stretched taut in a frame.

Squared laid work is made up of long stitches that form a lattice over which other stitches are worked. This basic structure is anchored by small, slanting stitches at each thread crossing. To form lattice, bring needle up at 1; take a long stitch to 2. Bring needle up at 3 below 2; insert at 4 below 1. Work stitches until area is covered, keeping spacing even. Lay vertical stitches over the horizontal ones the same way. Take small slanting stitch over each intersection. Start at upper left. Work across and back, up at A, down at B.

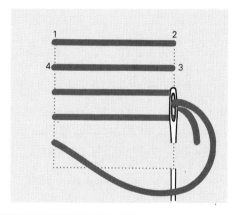

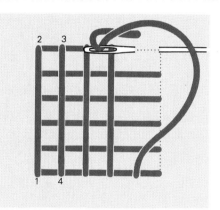

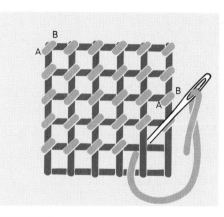

Variation 1. Here upright cross stitches are worked over alternate squares of the lattice made from the basic laid work shown above. Work entire lattice with one colour, cross stitches with a contrasting colour. Starting at upper left corner, bring needle up at 1; insert at 2. Come up at 3 and complete stitch at 4. Work the second row using the same numbered sequence, moving from right to left. Continue in this way, working each row until the laid work is filled.

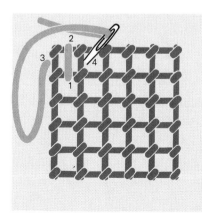

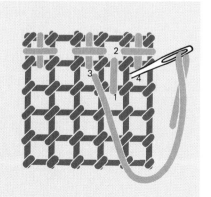

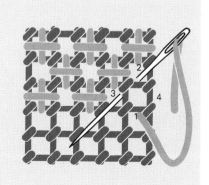

Variation 2. Here a series of four detached chain stitches is worked within a set of four lattice squares. Depending on the number of squares, the position and number of sets will vary. Make each chain stitch so that the anchoring stitch over the loop is at the centre of the four lattice squares. Bring needle up at 1; insert back into 1 and emerge at 2. Carry thread under point and pull through. With thread over loop, insert at 3. Work the next and subsequent stitches anti-clockwise until the set is complete.

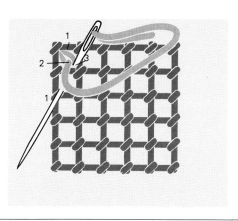 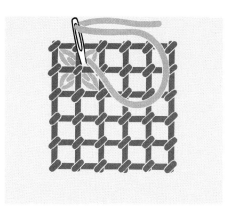 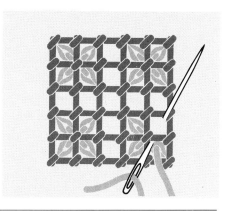

Variation 3. This time, diagonal threads are laid over basic threads, then anchored down at each intersection. Starting at top left corner of laid work, bring needle up at 1; insert at 2. Bring needle up at 3, two squares to the right. Take a diagonal stitch to 4, two squares below 1. Work remainder; keep spacing even. Lay diagonal threads in opposite direction. Start at top right and follow same sequence. At each crossing, take a small vertical stitch, A to B. Start at upper left corner; work across, then back, until all intersections are covered.

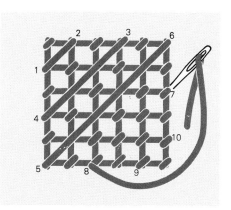 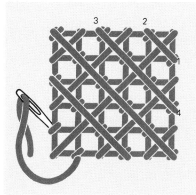 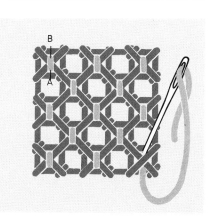

Diagonal laid work is made up of pairs of threads laid diagonally to form a lattice base. Each intersection is anchored down with four small straight stitches. To form lattice, bring needle up at 1 in upper left corner; insert diagonally at 2. Bring up at 3 near 2; take another stitch to 4. Work pairs of stitches back and forth, keeping spacing even. Then, starting at upper right corner, lay pairs of threads on the opposite diagonal. At each intersection, take four stitches, all out at A and in at centre point B. Work these sets across and then back.

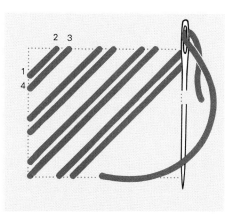 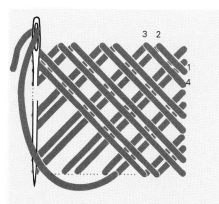 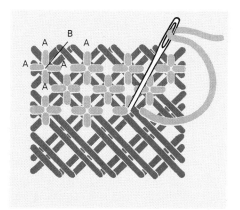

Embroidery stitches

Running stitches

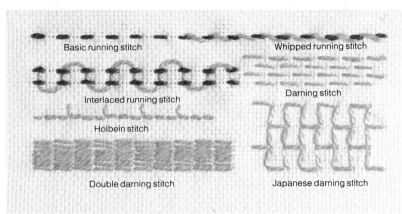

Basic running stitch

Whipped running stitch

Interlaced running stitch

Darning stitch

Holbein stitch

Double darning stitch

Japanese darning stitch

Running stitches would appear to be the simplest of all the stitch types to work, and in many ways they are. There is nothing at all complicated about the basic movements of the needle. Care is required, however, to keep the stitch lengths uniform. This is why the running stitch and its variants are frequently worked on fabrics that have an even weave, with every stitch length covering a predetermined number of fabric threads. Unlike the majority of embroidery stitches, almost all the running stitches can be worked by picking up several stitches on the needle before pulling the needle and thread through.

This speeds up the work considerably.

Basic running stitch is primarily used for outlining, and it is the basic stitch in quilting. Worked in rows with contrasting threads laced through it, it can also be used as a border or band. *Holbein* or *double running stitch* is often used for outlining. Carefully worked, a piece embroidered with only Holbein stitch can be reversible; right and wrong sides will be identical.

Darning stitches are usually used to fill a space. By changing the lengths and arrangements of the stitches, many different patterns are possible (see Blackwork, p. 54 and Pattern darning, p. 68).

Basic running stitch, the easiest outline stitch, can be same length on right and wrong sides or longer on right side. Work basic stitch right to left. Bring needle up at 1; down at 2. Pick up several stitches on needle before pulling it through. *For whipped variation,* weave contrasting thread through stitch base (second illustration); do not pick up fabric below. *For interlaced variation,* work two rows of running stitches and thread contrasting thread up and down through rows (last illustration).

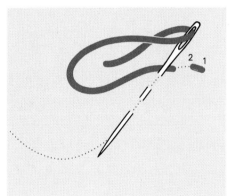

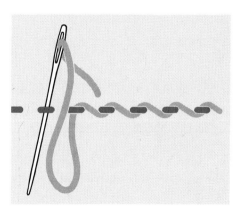

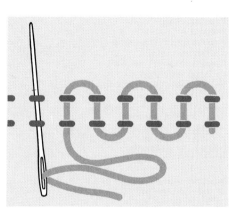

Darning stitch is basically several rows of running stitches of any desired length. Surface floats usually form a design like the type found in blackwork embroidery. We show a 'brick' design. Each row of running stitches consists of a long float on top with only a few fabric threads picked up by the needle. The long floats of each row are evenly stitched so that they lie just below short spaces of row directly above. Work rows as needed to fill area.

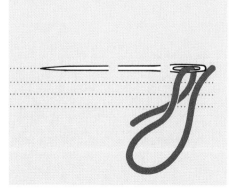

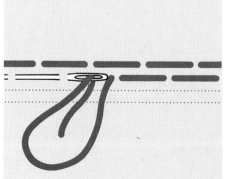

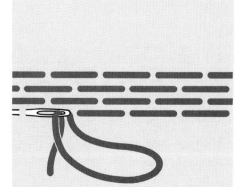

Holbein or double running stitch is an outline stitch used often in blackwork and Assisi embroidery. This stitch is worked with two journeys of running stitches. On first journey, work evenly spaced running stitches. Turn work and stitch second journey so top floats are stitched over spaces left by first journey; enter and come up at same holes.
If design has offshoot stitch, work it on first journey. Bring needle up at 3, base of stray stitch. Insert at 4; come up at 3 again. Continue to next stray stitch. Turn, and work back.

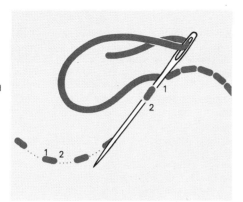
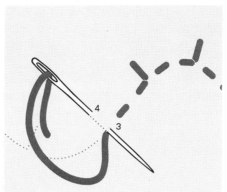
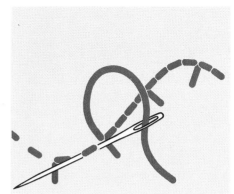

Double darning combines the techniques of both darning and Holbein stitches. This entails working several rows of evenly spaced Holbein stitches. To start, work the first journey of the first row with evenly spaced running stitches. Turn work, then stitch second journey over first so top floats are over spaces left by first journey. Work each subsequent row in the same manner, lining up stitches of each row directly below the stitches in the row above. Leave enough space between rows so the threads do not overlap each other.

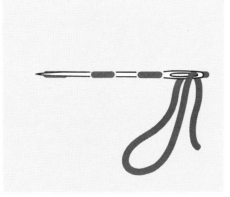
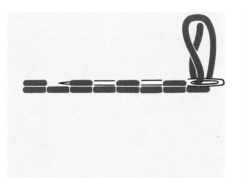

Japanese darning can be a filling stitch or a border. Work several rows of darning stitch in 'brick' pattern, but with more space between rows than in darning shown opposite. Work each row so the top float of each stitch is slightly longer than the intervening spaces. To connect rows, come up at 1 on top row. Insert at 2; come up at 3, with needle picking up fabric between 2 and 3. Continue, alternating pick-up stitches from row to row. Connect the subsequent rows in the same way until all have been joined.

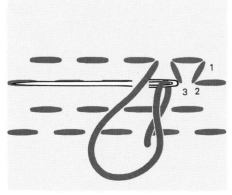

Embroidery stitches

Satin stitches

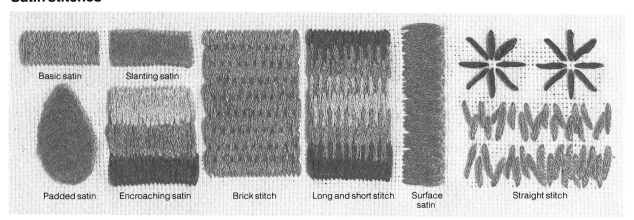

Basic satin

Slanting satin

Padded satin

Encroaching satin

Brick stitch

Long and short stitch

Surface satin

Straight stitch

This group of satin stitches is the most popular set of embroidery stitches for solidly filling in a design with a smooth surface. Although the main stitch movements are fairly simple, it still takes practice to get the floats to lie flat and close together, and the edges of the stitches to align evenly. When working satin stitches, be sure none of the fabric below shows through. An important aspect of satin stitching is the direction in which the stitches fall within a design. Decide this before starting; the stitch direction will influence the way the light reflects on the filled area, and will determine its ultimate look.

Basic satin stitch is a solid filling stitch that covers the design area with long, straight stitches placed close together. Care must be taken to keep the stitches smooth and at an even tension. This simple version of satin stitching is the basic stitch in Hardanger embroidery. The stitch is usually worked from left to right. Bring needle up at 1. Insert at 2 directly above; come up at 3 close to point 1. Continue until area is filled. The stabbling method of stitching (see p. 18) will help to keep the stitches even.

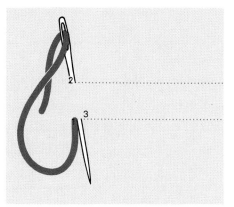

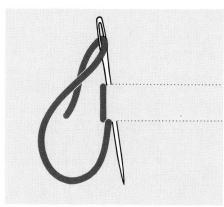

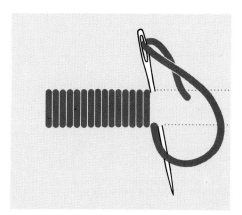

To slant satin stitches, start work in the centre of the shape to establish the angle of slant. Work across to fill one side, then start again at the centre and work across the other way to fill other side. When shape is large, slanting stitches tend to flatten out (becoming too horizontal) by the time you reach the end. To prevent this, work satin stitches so that needle is always inserted at upper edge (point 2) *very close* to preceding stitch; come up at 3 *slightly further* from exit point of preceding stitch.

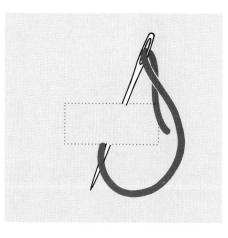

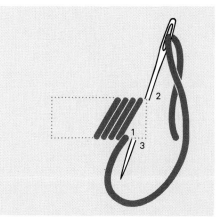

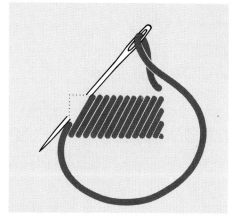

Padded satin stitch gives the same effect as the basic satin stitch, except that the stitched area is slightly raised for texture variation or design emphasis. The padded area consists of an outline of split stitches and two 'layers' of satin stitching. Work one row or split stitches (see p. 21) around the shape. Carefully work basic satin stitch horizontally across, covering the split stitches. Then work upper satin stitch layer in desired direction. Take special care to keep the outline edges even; work slowly.

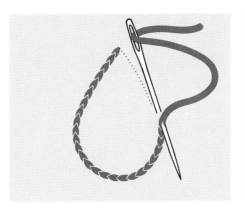 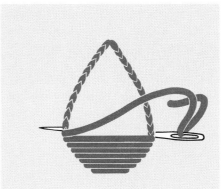 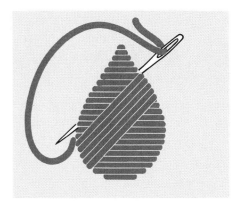

Encroaching satin stitch offers systematic colour shading within a shape. Several rows of basic satin stitches are worked to give an almost woven effect. The colours of the rows can go from dark to light. Work a basic satin stitch along first row. Start second row so that its first stitch falls between first two stitches in row above. Continue stitching second row so that stitches fall between the stitches above them. Work next rows the same way. If you use shaded thread, and want precise shading, start each row at the same colour section.

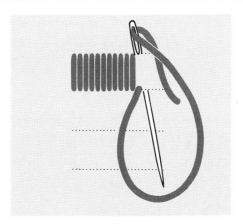 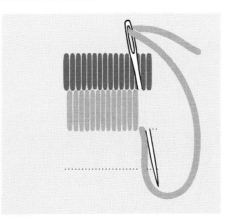 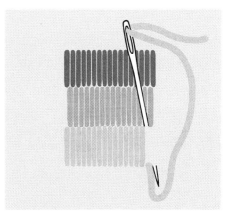

Brick stitch is a type of satin stitch with a texture like that of a woven basket. Stitching is done alternately left to right, then right to left. To work first row, alternate long and short satin stitches across; each short stitch should be approximately half the length of the long stitches. Work all other rows in long satin stitch. On last row, fill in the half-spaces with short satin stitches. Make sure that the top of each stitch touches the base of the stitches directly above it.

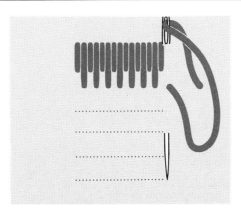 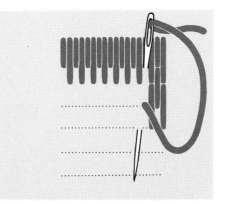 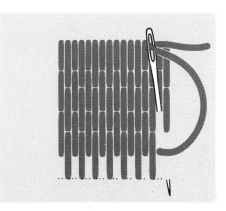

Embroidery stitches

Satin stitches

Long and short stitch is a popular stitch for shading areas in a design. The stitch is worked very similarly to brick stitch, but there is more stitch blending. Each stitch from the second row onwards pierces the stitch above it in the preceding row. Work first row as for brick stitch (preceding page). Change colour and work long satin stitches along second row, staggering them so top of each stitch splits base of stitch directly above. Work each subsequent row in this way. Fill in the last row with short satin stitches.

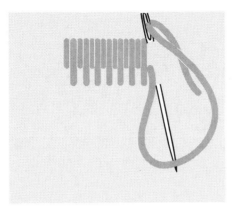 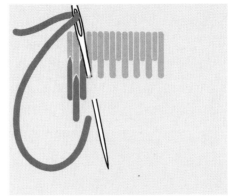 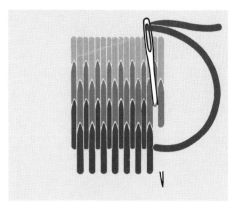

The direction in which long and short stitches fall is very important for proper shading effect. Before starting, decide direction stitches will take within each separate shape. Pencil in some direction lines. Here are three designs that have been partially worked with the long and short stitches running in different directions. Note the radiating coloured effect achieved in the first and last illustrations by fanning the first row of stitch colour.

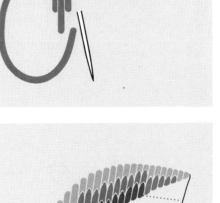 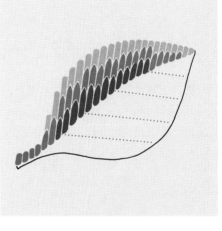 

Surface satin stitch is an economical way to obtain the look of the basic satin stitch; it eliminates the long floats on the wrong side. It needs care to get the stitches to lie close together. Use the stabbing motion (see p. 18) to work this stitch. Bring needle up at 1. Insert at 2 directly across; bring needle up at 3 as close as possible to 2 (no more than a fabric thread away). Insert needle at 4 directly across from 3. Or space the stitches slightly further apart and fill in with a second sequence of stitches for a smoother effect.

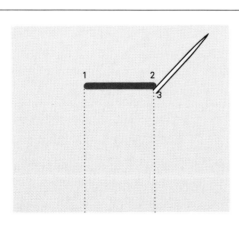 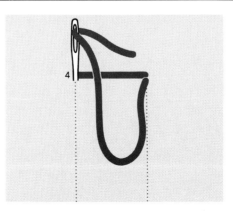 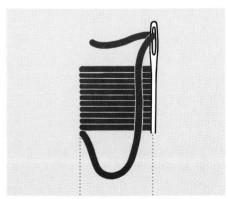

Straight stitch is a single satin stitch that can be of any length and worked in any direction. It can be used to cover straight design lines or scattered for an open filling. Be sure thread is not carried too far on wrong side between stitches. Worked in a circle (last illustration), the cluster of straight stitches resembles a stylised flower, the centre of which can be filled in with French knots (see p. 40). Bring needle up at 1; insert it at 2. Work as many as needed for desired design.

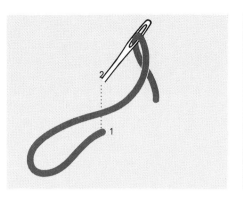

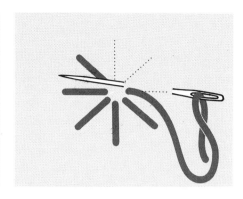

Weaving stitches

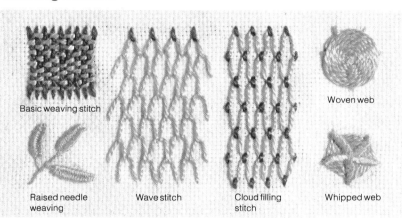

Basic weaving stitch

Raised needle weaving

Wave stitch

Cloud filling stitch

Woven web

Whipped web

The next embroidery stitch group, the weaving stitches, consists entirely of stitches based upon a network of threads that are first laid down and then woven over. The thread used for weaving may be the same or a contrasting colour. The effect, and therefore the choice, varies considerably from one stitch to another. The *basic weaving stitch,* for example, can fill an area solidly with its subtle texture; *raised needle weaving,* on the other hand, produces a particular motif, such as a leaf or petal. *Spiders' web stitches* are special in that the finished stitch assumes a definite circular shape. Both *wave stitch* and *cloud filling stitch* will serve as lacy fillings for different areas in a design. The filling can appear closed or quite open, however, depending on the placing of the base threads. The weight, too, affects stitch appearance, the same stitch looking very different in two different weights of thread. Experiment until you find the particular effect you want.

Although a pointed needle is used for laying down the base threads, it is recommended that you exchange it for a tapestry needle when you come to the weaving portion of these stitches. This will help to avoid piercing the fabric or splitting the laid threads.

Basic weaving stitch is a solid filling stitch with a basket-like texture. Lay down the vertical threads first, working right to left. Bring needle up at 1; insert at 2 directly above and come up at 3 on left. Insert at 4 and repeat for as many threads as needed. Change to tapestry needle. Starting at upper right corner, come up at A and weave across, going over and under alternate vertical threads. Insert needle at B; come up at C for next horizontal run. Continue to weave vertical threads.

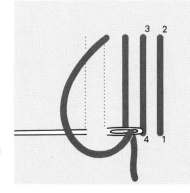

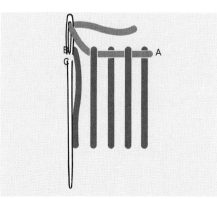

Embroidery stitches

Weaving stitches

Raised needle weaving is a weaving stitch that lies on top of fabric with only laid threads attached. Bring needle out at 1. Insert at 2 directly below; emerge at 1. Insert needle at 2 again and bring needle up at 1. Change to a tapestry needle; begin weaving over and under the two laid threads alternately without picking up any fabric below. Continue to work back and forth over the laid threads until they are completely covered. Take care to keep the tension even so the shape of the stitches is not distorted.

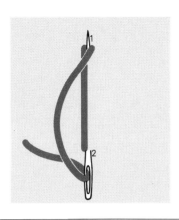 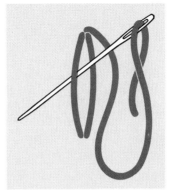 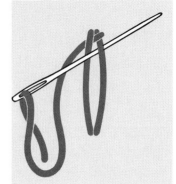 

Wave stitch is a lacy filling stitch that gives a honeycomb effect. Depending on the spacing of the stitches, this lace-like effect can look open or closed. To start, work a row of small, vertical satin stitches that are evenly spaced. Come up at 1; insert at 2. At end of row, bring needle up at 3, below and to right of last satin stitch. Pass needle back under satin stitch without picking up any fabric below; insert at 4. Bring needle up right next to point 4 and repeat the sequence until all satin stitches are threaded.

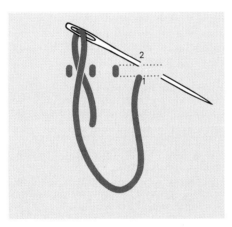 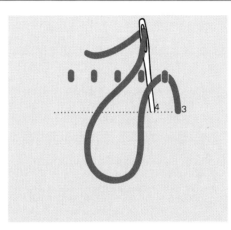 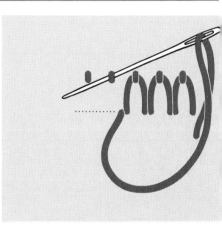

To work next row, bring needle up at 5 slightly to the left of the last stitch above. Pass needle under stitch above without picking up fabric. Insert at 6. Bring needle up right next to point 6 and repeat the sequence across, this time slipping needle under the pairs of stitch bases directly above. On following row, bring needle up at 7 directly under end stitch of first weaving row, and end at point 8, directly under end stitch of first weaving row. Work subsequent rows the same way, passing needle under the stitch bases in row directly above.

 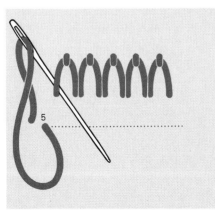 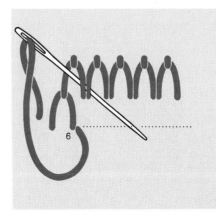 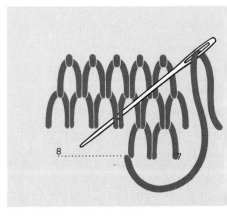

Cloud filling stitch is much like the wave stitch in texture. To start, work several rows of small, vertical, evenly spaced satin stitches as shown on the right. Change to tapestry needle and contrasting thread. Bring needle up at A; lace thread back and forth through satin stitches of first two rows. End lacing at B, securing thread at back. Lace second and third rows (C to D) and all subsequent pairs of rows. Different impressions can be achieved with contrasting threads and by varying spacing.

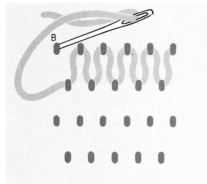
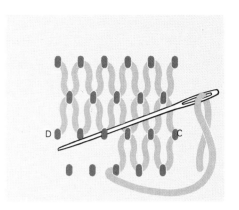

Spiders' webs are embroidered circular motifs that can be used as design accents or to represent stylised flowers. Spokes of the web are laid, then *woven over and under* for a smooth surface or *whipped* to produce a pronounced rib. Before starting, divide circle into nine equal parts; mentally number each. Bring needle up at spoke 1. Insert at 4 and bring out at centre; carry thread under needle and pull through. Insert at 7 and bring out at 9. Insert at 3 and bring out at centre; carry thread under needle and pull through. Insert at 6 and bring out at 8.

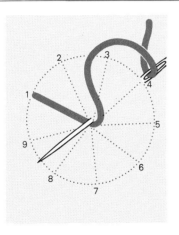
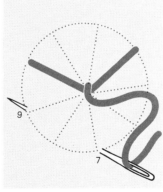
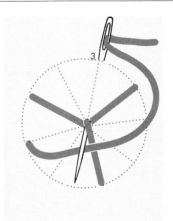
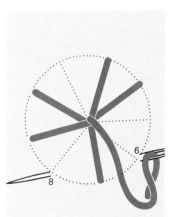

Insert needle at spoke 2 and bring out at centre; carry thread under needle, pull through. To complete last spoke, insert needle at 5 and come up at centre. To *weave* over spokes, start from centre and pass needle over and under spokes, moving around and outwards anti-clockwise until spokes are covered. To *whip* over spokes (last illustration), carry needle under and back over a spoke, then under that spoke and next spoke ahead. Work around, always moving needle back over one spoke and forward under two in a backstitch until all spokes are covered.

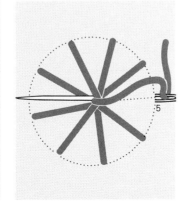
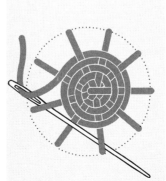
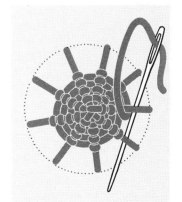

Finishing embroidered pieces

Cleaning, pressing and blocking embroidery

Cleaning

Because of all the handling involved in the embroidering process, your finished piece may get very dirty and need cleaning before it is pressed or blocked. Embroidered pieces made with washable fabrics and threads can simply be washed as illustrated below. Swish the embroidery around in the cool, soapy water – never scrub embroidery harshly – rinse thoroughly, and roll in a towel to blot up the excess water. If the piece is not washable, you can use a good stain remover – which you have first tested on a scrap of fabric – or take the piece to a reliable dry-cleaner.

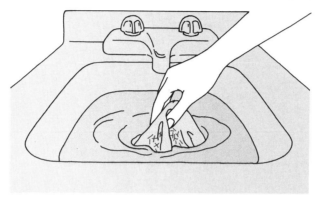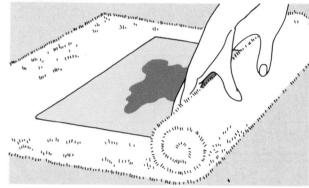

Gently wash the embroidered piece in cool water and mild soap. Rinse thoroughly (do not wring or twist); **roll in towel** to absorb excess moisture.

Pressing

When an embroidered piece is completed, it must be either **pressed** or **blocked** to help remove any wrinkles and to straighten fabric distortions that may have been caused by embroidering. If a piece is not seriously distorted, pressing is usually sufficient. Pressing, rather than blocking, is also recommended for embroidered clothing. Before pressing, pad the ironing board with a folded towel. If your board is too narrow to take the work satisfactorily, lay the towel over your blocking board. Place the embroidered piece face down and cover it with a cloth. If the article has been washed (see above) and is still damp, you can use a dry cloth; if the piece is dry, use a damp cloth. Press very lightly over the embroidered area, letting the iron just touch the cloth. Press surrounding fabric in usual way.

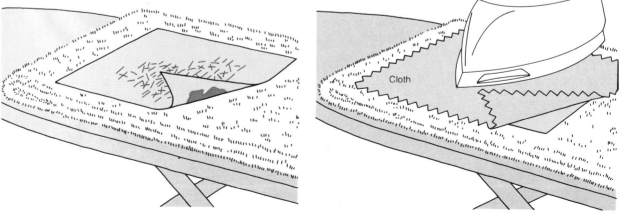

To press an embroidered piece, lay it face down on a padded ironing board, and cover with a cloth. **Press lightly** so that iron barely touches the cloth.

Blocking

Blocking is a corrective process in which embroidery pieces are stretched over a board to remove fabric wrinkles and distortions. To make a blocking board, see below. If you would like to pad the board, cut an old mattress cover into pieces to fit the board, and place a couple of them between the board and the covering of muslin.

To block embroidery, first soak the piece in cold water. If the stitches are flat, lay the piece face down on the board; if many stitches are raised and highly textured, lay it face up to prevent crushing. Stretch the fabric and hold it in place with heavy-duty T-pins or drawing pins placed close together. Pieces that cannot be soaked should be stretched dry. Moisten areas around embroidery with a damp sponge, and use tip of iron to press moistened areas lightly; let fabric dry before removing.

If the piece has been worked on a frame it should not require stretching.

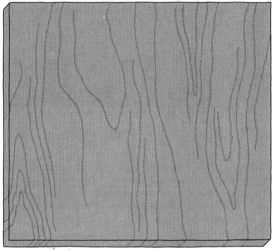

1. To make blocking board, buy a piece of 1.5 cm thick pine or soft composition board that is approximately 60 cm by 60 cm.

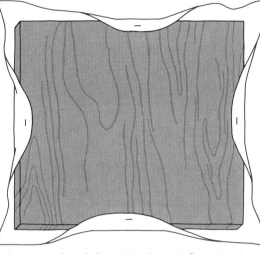

2. Cut a piece of muslin 5 cm wider all around. Centre board over fabric, and stretch fabric over edge, stapling at centre of each side.

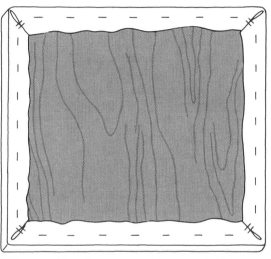

3. Working out from the centres, stretch and staple fabric along each edge. Neatly fold excess fabric at corners and staple.

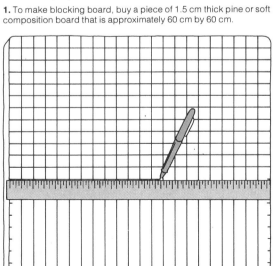

4. Turn board to right side and mark off a 2 cm grid, using an indelible marking pen that will not run when wet.

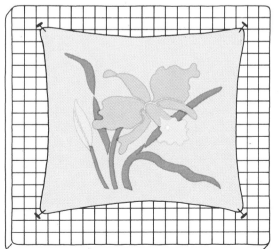

5. Soak embroidered piece in cold water and lay on top of board, face up or down as explained above. Pin at each corner.

6. Pull sides out to desired measurements, using grid as a guide, and pin in place. Leave it to dry before removing.

Blackwork embroidery

Introduction

Blackwork is a special category of counted thread embroidery in which repetitive patterns are used to fill design areas. It is called blackwork because, traditionally, black silk thread was worked on white linen.

Blackwork is said to have originated in Spain, becoming very popular in England during the 16th century when Catherine of Aragon married Henry VIII. At that time, blackwork appeared on clothing and pillow covers.

The play of one diaper pattern upon another creates dark, medium and light areas within a design; a mixture of all three tones adds interest to a piece. Today, blackwork patterns are used in working two different types of designs: **block designs,** in which the patterns themselves form a simple geometric shape; and **free designs,** in which the patterns are used to fill predetermined shapes in a design.

Blackwork is done on even-weave fabric (see p. 7), typically even-weave linen or Hardanger fabric. For exact pattern repetition, stitches are counted over a precise number of threads. The more threads there are per centimetre of fabric, the smaller (and darker) the embroidered blackwork area will be.

Stranded cotton is usually used in blackwork; depending on the weave of the fabric, the number of strands can vary. Finer pearl cottons and cotton à broder are also suitable. Although black thread on white linen is the traditional colour choice, other colours can be used to give blackwork a more modern look. Brown thread on beige linen or deep blue on eggshell are popular (see examples on the right). Metallic threads add richness to a design.

Because blackwork is worked over an exact number of threads, the needle must go between threads rather than pierce them. For this purpose, fine tapestry needles are best. Select a size that corresponds to your thread.

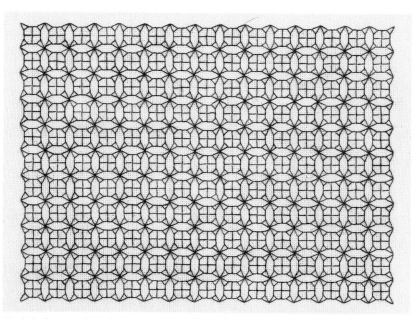

Block designs consist of simple geometric units formed by the blackwork patterns themselves.

Free designs make use of outline stitches with blackwork fillings.

Basic stitches

Blackwork patterns are built upon a few basic embroidery stitches worked over a definite number of threads. The stitches that are used most often are shown below. Included are **backstitch, Holbein** and **running stitch, double cross stitch** and **Algerian eye stitch.**

In addition to the stitches that create the patterns, other stitches are often used as embellishments to add textural interest and variety to the overall design or to outline shapes. The free design on the opposite page features such supplementary stitching. One excellent contrast to the intricate blackwork lines is a solidly filled area; **satin stitch** will provide a smooth, solid filling where such an effect is wanted. To add definition to a free shape, outline it with a linear embroidery stitch. **Stem stitch, chain stitch** and **couching stitches** are all good for this purpose.

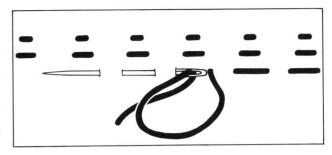

Darning stitch is often used alone in blackwork patterns. A running stitch worked in parallel rows, its floats may be any length. Stitch rows create the patterns.

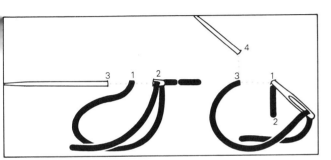

Basic backstitch is worked right to left. Bring needle out at 1, go in at 2 and out at 3. To stitch corners, come up at 1, take a backstitch at 2 and come up at 3. Insert at 1; come up at 4; re-insert at 3 to complete stitch.

 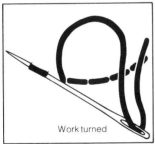

Work turned

Holbein stitch is worked in two runs. The first consists of a simple running stitch. The return run is made along the same stitching line with running stitch filling in spaces left from the first.

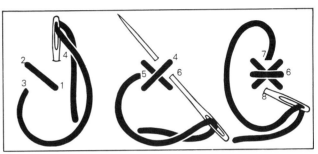

Double cross stitch is star-like. To work, bring needle up at 1, go in at 2 and out at 3 below 2. Enter at 4, come up at 5 between 2 and 3. Insert at 6 across from 5; come up at 7 between 2 and 4. Insert at 8 below to complete stitch.

Algerian eye stitch produces an eyelet effect. To work, bring the needle up at 1 and insert at centre, A. Bring out at 2 and insert at A. Continue to work in clockwise direction until all points are stitched.

Additional stitches

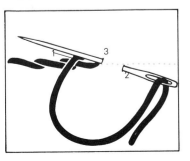

Stem stitch is worked left to right. Bring needle out at 1. Insert at 2 and bring out at 3. The distance between 1-3 and 3-2 is the same. Repeat sequence for next stitch. Keep length of stitches even.

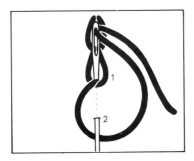

Chain stitch is worked as follows. Bring needle up at 1. Holding thread down to left of 1, re-insert needle at 1, bring out at 2, looping thread around needle point. Pull needle through and repeat the sequence.

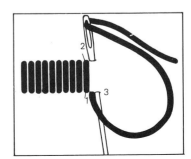

Satin stitch is used to fill small areas. Bring needle up at 1, down at 2. Emerge at 3 right next to 1. Repeat same sequence until area is filled. Keep thread smooth and even.

Blackwork embroidery

Examples of blackwork patterns

Blackwork patterns consist of repetitive geometric motifs made from basic embroidery stitches. The original blackwork patterns probably were derived from Arabic embroidery designs. Later, when blackwork reached the height of its popularity in 16th-century England, the original geometric patterns were influenced by English design. At that time, fruits and figures were used as repeated motifs, with twining stems giving a cohesive look to the design. Elizabethan portraits of both men and women show this kind of blackwork pattern covering sleeves and collars. Some patterns are reminiscent of engravings or wrought iron work.

Even in the 16th century, blackwork was not always done in black thread on white or cream linen. Sometimes gold and black thread were used together in one piece. Even red thread, on occasion, was substituted for black.

We have selected 12 patterns to illustrate the range of possibilities. The number of patterns, however, is infinite. They are simple to design on your own (see p. 61) or to adapt from an existing design. Look at fabric prints or mosaic tile designs for inspiration. Or choose any blackwork pattern that appeals to you and simply change its scale or the thickness of the thread.

Each pattern will tend to have a dark, medium or light tone according to the relative openness or compactness of its lines. Note the differences on the sampler. A sampler like this one will serve as a pattern dictionary for future use and will provide you with practice in working the patterns. Any pattern can be adapted to either free designs or block. The best pattern combinations are those that create textural contrast.

To show the order of steps necessary to work the patterns, each sequence begins in black and continues in colour. On the grids, the spaces between dots represent individual fabric threads.

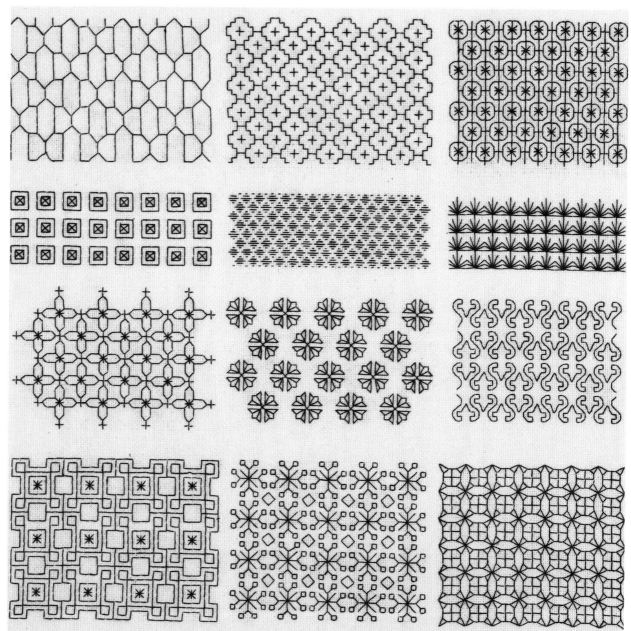

Representative sampler of 12 blackwork patterns illustrates the three tones of light, medium and dark.

This light, honeycomb pattern is worked completely in *backstitch* or *Holbein*. Work the pattern from left to right, stitching vertical rows in stitch lengths as indicated on grid (second illustration). For backstitch, work first line from top down, and second line (shown in colour) from bottom up. Continue in this way until desired area is completely filled. For Holbein stitch, work first stage of each line from top down, and second stage from bottom up.

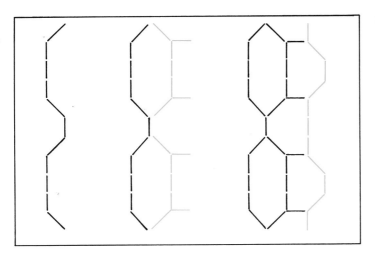

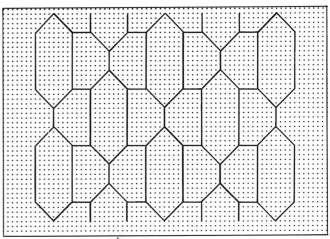

Step design is darker than the honeycomb because its lines are closer, its motif smaller. Work the basic shapes in *backstitch* in the sequence shown. Then fill centres with a single, vertical *cross stitch*. This pattern can be used as a border or filling.

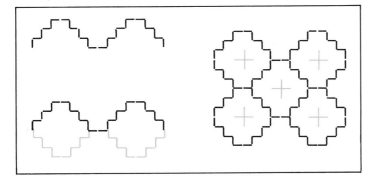

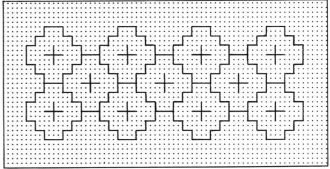

Octagonal trellis is a compact pattern worked in *backstitch* and *cross stitch*. The vertical lines and octagons are worked in backstitch. The octagons are then filled with cross stitch. The horizontal stitches add a third arm to the crosses and connect the octagons.

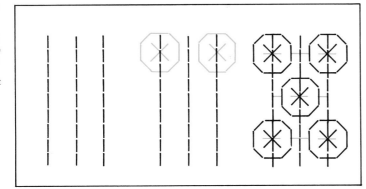

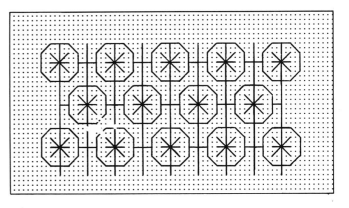

Blackwork embroidery

Examples of blackwork patterns

Delicate diamonds are worked entirely in *darning stitch*. The top floats, worked in rows, create the patterns. To begin, work the top row of either pattern from right to left, spacing stitches as shown on grid. Work subsequent rows, following stitch pattern, until desired area is filled.

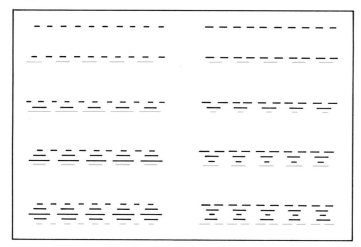

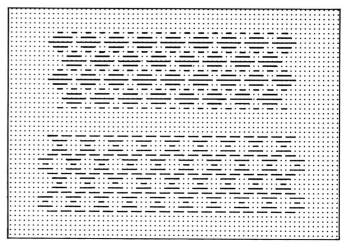

Dark fern pattern is made of closely stitched motifs. Each motif is worked like *Algerian eye stitch*, coming up at the end of each line and entering at same centre hole. Work across one row and return on next row until area is filled. Note stitch lengths as indicated on grid.

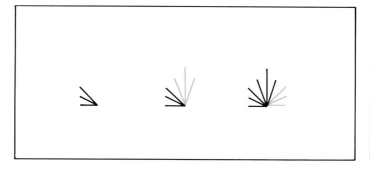

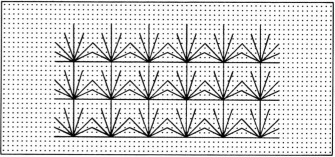

A simple geometric shape like this filled double square can be given a light or dark tone depending on its filling. To work this pattern, stitch the squares in *backstitch* and fill with *cross stitch*. For a darker pattern, use *double cross stitch*. Work blocks closer together, or use a heavier thread.

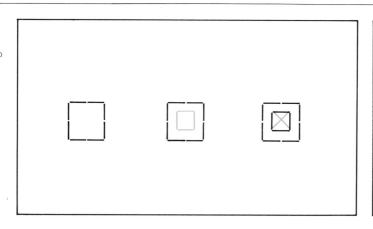

This Greek scroll, though it looks complex, is easy to work. *Backstitch* or *Holbein* can be used. Work the first row as shown. For the next row, invert motif to create a mirror-image effect. This pattern can be used as a filling or as a border.

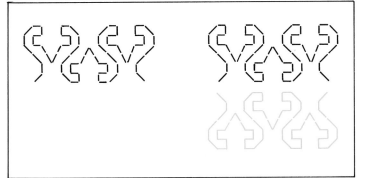 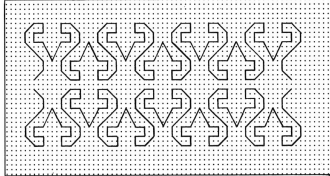

Crossed star motif is composed of a network of intersecting stars. Begin each star with a central *double cross stitch.* Add the points in *backstitch* and join the stars with a single vertical-horizontal *cross stitch* at each point.

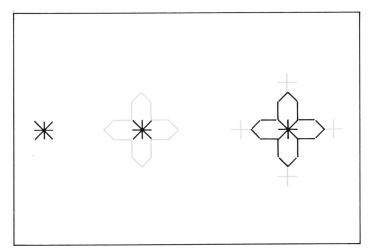 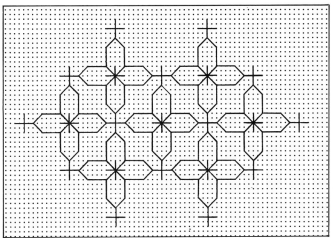

Flower arrangement. To work this pattern, stitch centre *cross stitch* of each group, suitably spaced. Then work the outline of one motif, in *backstitch,* adding the detail lines last. Work the other three motifs in the same way.

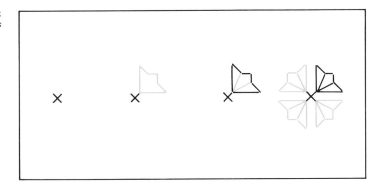 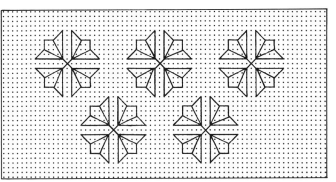

Blackwork embroidery

Examples of blackwork patterns

Scattered snowflakes. Work snowflake centre in *Algerian eye stitch*. Then work the adjoining lines and shapes in *backstitch*. When all rows of pattern are complete, add the diamond shapes in backstitch.

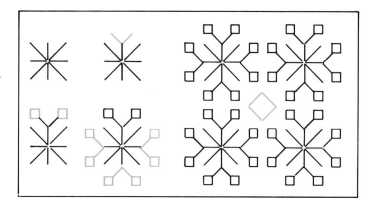

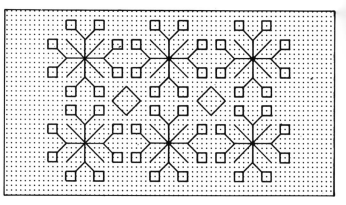

Stacked 'H' shapes are worked from the outside. The main motifs are worked in *backstitch* (see p. 55 for the way to work corners). Fill in the centres of the 'H' shapes with *Algerian eye stitch*.

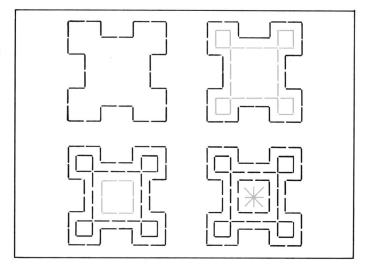

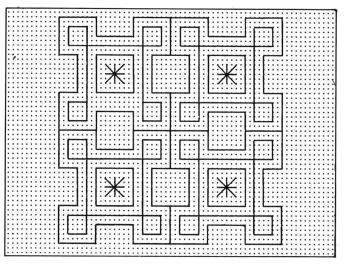

Stained-glass pattern. Though the lines look intricate, this pattern is easy to work. Begin by stitching a *backstitch* cross. Add an octagonal ring and four corner triangles (all backstitch).

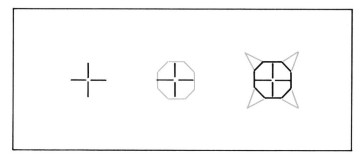

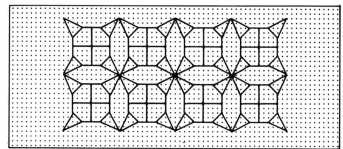

Creating your own blackwork pattern

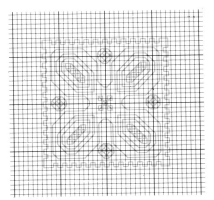

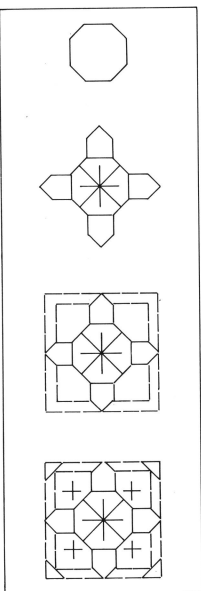

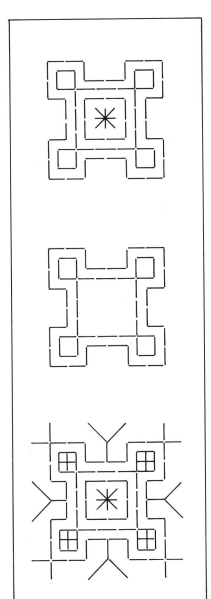

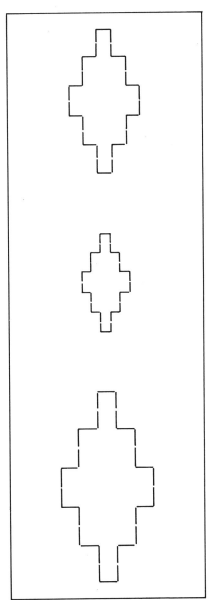

A geometric motif from a fabric print or a ceramic tile can be used by 'squaring' all curved lines, with the help of graph paper. To suit blackwork technique, all parts of the design must take a horizontal, vertical or diagonal direction.

Develop your own pattern from any simple geometric shape, adding lines and other shapes to fill in or extend the original shape. Pattern above combines Algerian eye stitch, backstitch and cross stitch.

Modify an existing blackwork pattern to your taste. Simplify the motif by removing some of its lines. Or add lines for a larger or more complex pattern. Algerian eye stitch, backstitch and cross stitch are used above.

Change the scale of an existing pattern to give it a new look. Enlarge the motif by lengthening the stitches. To make the motif smaller than the original, shorten the stitches. Motif shown is worked in backstitch, over 2, 4 or 6 threads.

Blackwork embroidery

Working blackwork in block designs

When working a blackwork piece to form a block or all-over design (see block design on p. 54); the blackwork pattern must be symmetrically placed. To accomplish this you must carefully measure and divide the area to be stitched.

First determine the approximate size the finished blackwork design is to be. Then cut even-weave fabric on grain to the dimensions of the projected design plus 10 cm on all sides. Bind or finish the raw edges of the cut fabric to prevent fraying as you embroider (see p. 14). Count the threads within the area to be worked and mark the perimeters clearly. Since blackwork patterns are worked from the centre out, the centre point of the design must be located and marked. Place the initial motif in relation to the centre point so that as many *whole motifs* as possible fit into the worked area. This positioning is particularly important if the motifs are large.

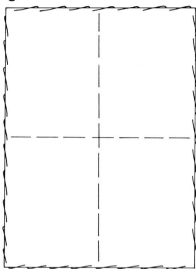

1. Fold fabric in half vertically; tack along centre line with thread. Fold fabric in half across and tack along that centre line. Intersecting tacking lines mark centre of fabric.

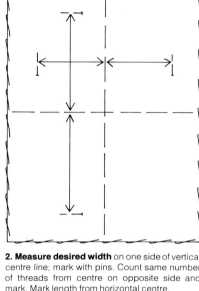

2. Measure desired width on one side of vertical centre line; mark with pins. Count same number of threads from centre on opposite side and mark. Mark length from horizontal centre.

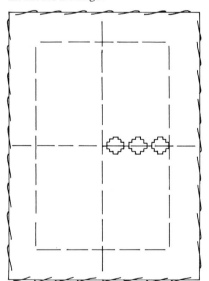

3. Tack along pinned lines for perimeter of design. Start from centre point and work one horizontal row of pattern outwards from vertical centre line. Work other half in opposite direction.

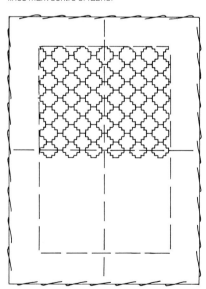

4. To fill remaining area, repeat rows of pattern above and below first row. Using it as a guide, subsequent rows can be worked from edge to edge, rather than from centre out.

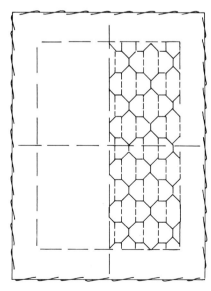

5. If the selected pattern is worked vertically, stitch first row out from horizontal centre line. To fill remaining area, stitch subsequent rows, using first completed row as a guide.

POSITIONING LARGE MOTIF

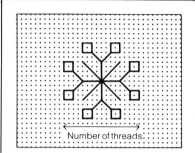

If a motif is large, whether it will be worked horizontally or vertically, as many motifs as possible should be worked on a line. To accomplish this, count fabric threads in a row, then fabric threads in one motif. Divide number of fabric threads by the number in one motif.

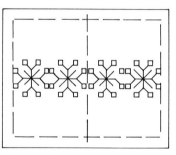

If the result is an even number, start motif *at* centre line, working a complete motif on either side of centre.

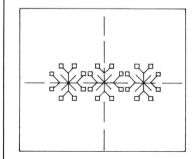

If result is an odd number, work half a motif *on either side* of centre line so that one full motif is centred.

Working blackwork fillings

When blackwork patterns are used as fillings within freely drawn shapes, they must be selected carefully. Choose patterns that have different tones of light and dark, distinct enough so that the shapes in the piece do not become blurred. When combined thoughtfully, the lights and darks can add depth and interest to a free design.

In choosing a pattern to fill any shape, consider the size of the shape in relation to the scale of the pattern. Make sure that there is enough space within the area to repeat the motif several times. Otherwise, the pattern will not be shown to its best advantage.

In addition to the basic stitches used to work patterns, consider working other embroidery stitches. Use *chain stitch*, *stem stitch* or *couching stitches* to emphasise and outline shapes that need definition. Or incorporate very dark areas of contrast into the design by filling small shapes with *satin stitch*.

1. Trace or draw design on heavy tracing paper. Colour in different tones of grey to represent light, medium and dark patterns. Arrange them for balance and contrast. Select the patterns that best represent the greys in the drawing.

2. Cut out even-weave fabric on grain 10 cm wider on all sides than the desired finished size of design. Bind or finish the raw edges of the fabric to prevent fraying while the design is being worked (see p. 14). Transfer the design to the fabric (pp. 14–15).

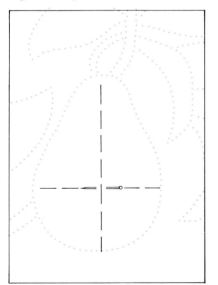

3. Determine approximate centre of each shape to be filled; mark with a pin. Block designs must be centred by thread counting; centre of a free shape can be determined by eye.

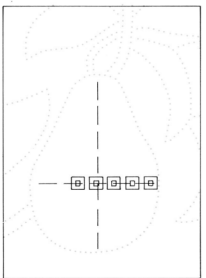

4. Start pattern at centre, working the row out to marked edges. At edges where a whole motif may not fit, use part of a motif, perhaps shortening stitches, to keep pattern within outline.

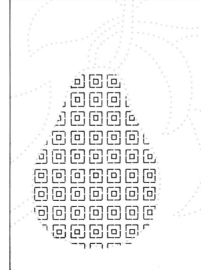

5. Repeat the pattern rows, using the first completed row as a guide. As before, at edges where a whole motif does not fit, work a partial motif, shortening stitches as necessary.

6. When all shapes in design have been filled, outline them, using such stitches as *stem stitch*, *chain stitch* or *couching stitches*. Fill in solid areas with *satin stitch*.

Cross stitch embroidery

Introduction

Cross stitch is a traditional type of embroidery which is adaptable to either simple or intricate designs. Cross stitch designs are often worked exclusively in basic cross stitch, as on the right, though variations of the stitch can also be used.

Cross stitch can be worked on almost any fabric suitable for embroidery. The even-weave types are especially good because their even threads help guide the stitches. Gingham is popular for cross stitch for a similar reason – its squares form a natural grid (see p. 7).

Stranded cotton is the usual choice for working cross stitch, but other embroidery threads can be used. Just be sure the thread you select is compatible with the weight of your embroidery fabric.

Choose a needle according to your fabric: a tapestry needle for an even-weave, to slip between threads; for other fabrics, a sharp-pointed needle (crewel or chenille) to pierce the fabric. To keep stitch tension even, it is best to use an embroidery hoop or frame.

Versatile basic cross stitch fills shapes, forms geometric motifs and outlines designs.

Forming the basic cross stitch

Basic cross stitch can be formed in two ways. It can be worked **in rows** of even, slanted stitches, with one arm of the crosses laid down in one movement, the other in a second, return movement.

Cross stitches can also be worked **one at a time.** Work cross stitches in a row when they are adjacent in a design. When they are scattered, it is best to work them singly; this way no long threads will be trailed on the wrong side. Make sure that the top threads all lie in the same direction. This is important to obtain the even, neat look that is characteristic of cross stitch.

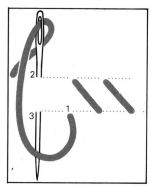
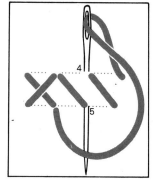

Cross stitches in a row. Starting on the right, come up at 1, insert at 2 and come up at 3. At end of row, work back, inserting at 4, coming up at 5.

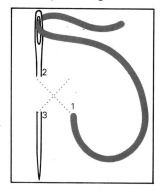
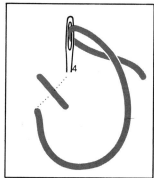

To work one cross stitch at a time. Bring needle up at 1, insert at 2 and come up at 3 below. To complete, insert needle at 4 above 1.

Cross stitch guides

There are two sources for cross stitch designs, **hot-iron transfers** and **charted designs**. Hot-iron transfers can be applied to any smooth, tightly woven fabric. Use charted designs on any fabric that offers a natural grid (even-weaves, or plain weaves with an even surface pattern, such as gingham).

With an iron-on transfer, your finished embroidery will be the same size as the transfer. If you use a charted design, finished size will depend on the number of fabric threads or surface lines you work over.

Charted designs (both the coloured key and symbol key types) are printed on a grid. Each square in the grid represents a single cross stitch. The scale of each stitch is your choice.

With iron-on transfers for cross stitch, simple crosses indicate stitch position.

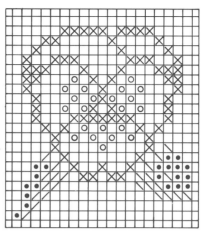

In charted designs with symbol keys, symbols represent stitch position and colour.

Charted designs with colour keys show stitch position and colour with coloured squares.

Natural grids

Fabrics with natural grids (even-weaves, and plain weaves with even surface patterns) are ideal for cross stitch. With charted designs, fabrics of this type are essential. When the weave pattern is large, as in Binca fabric, each cross stitch can cover one thread inter- section. When it is smaller, as in Har- danger fabric, each cross stitch can cover several fabric strands or thread intersections. Be sure each stitch crosses the same number of fabric threads hori- zontally and vertically.

When a fabric does not have a natural grid, a **single-thread canvas** can supply one. Choose a suitable size, making sure the mesh is not interlocked, and tack it to the embroidery fabric. Work the cross stitch design over the canvas grid. When the design is completed, remove the tacking stitches and trim the excess canvas close to the design without cut- ting into the cross stitches. Carefully draw out the canvas threads with tweez- ers. Start from one corner and pull all parallel threads in one direction. Then, working from another corner, pull out the remaining threads.

Cross stitch on Binca fabric shows each stitch worked over one thread group.

Cross stitch on a fine even-weave shows each stitch worked over two threads.

Canvas, tacked to embroidery fabric, can substi- tute for a fabric grid.

When the design is finished, the canvas threads are pulled out with tweezers.

Cross stitch embroidery

Cross stitch on gingham

Gingham is a highly popular fabric for cross stitch because of its natural grid. One cross is worked within each square, which keeps stitches uniform.

Any charted design that requires a fabric with a natural grid can be worked on gingham, but some designs are particularly effective on this fabric. The three tones of gingham (dark, medium and white) can be used to advantage (see below). A motif worked on only the dark squares will create a different effect, for example, from the same motif worked on the medium or the white squares.

Gingham comes in check sizes from one to three per centimetre. Since the check size determines the size of each cross, the larger the squares, the larger the overall design.

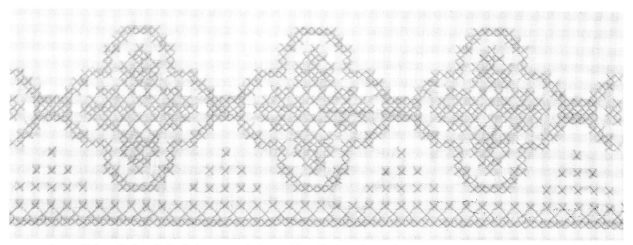

Cross stitch on gingham design features a repeated geometric motif, a favourite use of the technique and ideal for decorative borders.

Crosses worked on the dark squares enhance the contrast between whites and darks.

Crosses worked on the white squares give a one-tone look to the gingham.

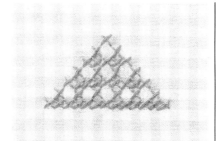

Crosses on both dark and white squares make shape more solid, whites more emphatic.

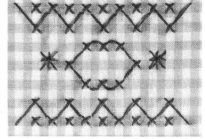

Variations of the basic cross stitch can be incorporated into the main motifs of a design or used to embellish a border pattern. The variations above are *herringbone stitch* (p. 34) and *double cross stitch* (p. 33).

Working sample motif

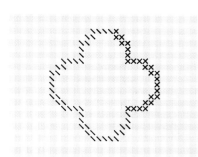

Individual flowers are stitched separately. Work outline as a row (in two journeys).

Next fill in centre petals, working one petal at a time, again as a row.

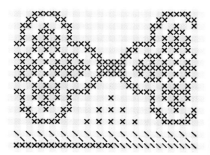

Work connecting blocks and border stitches as rows. Stitch triangle crosses one at a time.

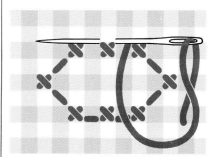

Work medallion with basic cross stitches, adding running stitches to connect them.

Assisi embroidery

Assisi embroidery is a variation of basic cross stitch, in which design areas are left open and the background filled with cross stitch. Designs are usually outlined with Holbein stitch (see p. 45). Details and highlights within the open forms are also worked with either Holbein or cross stitch.

The technique is named after the town in northern Italy where it originated. (Assisi is also the birthplace of St Francis, founder of the Franciscan order.) A revival of this traditional Italian embroidery took place at the beginning of this century. The designs were adapted from centuries-old embroidered pieces preserved by local churches. The motifs in these early 20th-century pieces were of primitively drawn animals. As the embroidery became more popular and greater variety of design was needed, elaborate patterns were adapted from the woodcarvings in the churches of Assisi. The adaptations include animals, figures, geometric and floral motifs. Traditionally, only one colour was used. Today, colours can be mixed. A particularly effective way of combining colour is to use one for filling and another for outline and detail.

Most cross stitch charts can be adapted for Assisi work. Simply select designs with strong shapes and reverse the open and filled areas.

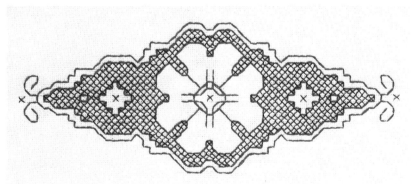

The first Assisi designs were naively drawn animal shapes. Later, the designs were refined into more delicate shapes, abstract, floral and geometric shapes, and intertwining figures.

To work an Assisi piece, first stitch the outline of the shape in *Holbein stitch*, worked as two journeys of running stitches. On the first journey, stitch evenly spaced running stitches. Work the second journey so that top floats are stitched over the spaces left by the first journey. Enter and come up at the same holes. When the outline is complete, fill in the background areas with cross stitch, worked in rows (see p. 64).

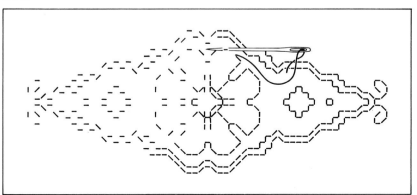

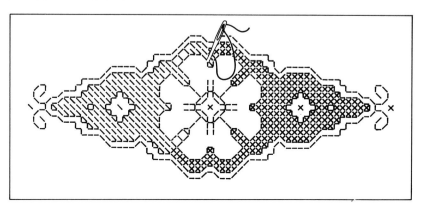

Pattern darning

Introduction to embroidery
Motifs
Basic stitch movements
Working pattern darning

Introduction

The type of pattern darning shown here is traditionally worked on Huckaback linen, a towelling fabric with well-defined vertical floats in the weave. This fabric is now difficult to obtain, but with a little ingenuity the method can be adapted to even-weave or to honeycomb fabric.

A look at the magnified insets on these two pages will show how pattern darning looks on even-weave fabric. It does require some planning if you wish to stagger some rows (see bottom left motif, p. 69). As even-weave does not have floats already spaced out, you will have to devise your own system. You could, for instance, pick up every fourth vertical thread in a straight row of darning. This would leave three clear threads in between (an odd number) which makes it possible to stagger the next row by picking up the middle of the three threads. This would not be possible if you picked up the third or fifth thread, leaving an even number of threads in between.

In honeycomb fabric, the vertical floats lie in straight rows up and down, with horizontal floats in alternate rows. To follow some of the stitch diagrams on pp. 69–71 you will have, on alternate lines, to pick up two warp threads which lie between the horizontal floats.

Threads used for pattern darning are usually pearl cotton and stranded cotton; sometimes Persian wool and soft embroidery cottons are used. Because the needle picks up the floats rather than piercing the fabric, a tapestry needle, in a size that suits your thread, is recommended. An embroidery hoop is not needed. Designs for pattern darning are usually geometric shapes, used as a *single motif*, a *border*, *all-over or repetitive patterns* or *stylised figures*. Examples appear on the far right, with drawings that show the order of working each type. For drawings of the basic stitch movements, see p. 70.

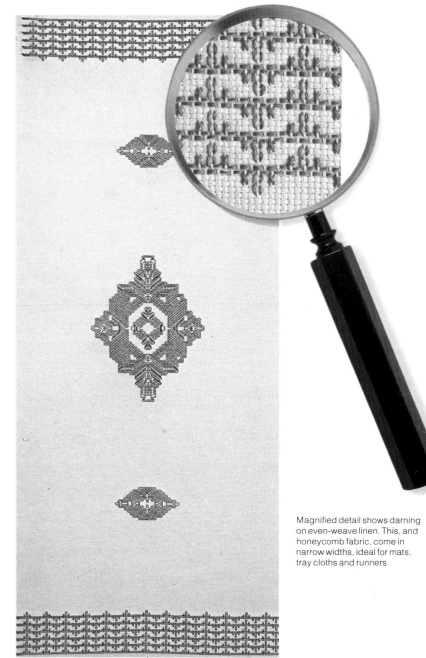

Magnified detail shows darning on even-weave linen. This, and honeycomb fabric, come in narrow widths, ideal for mats, tray cloths and runners.

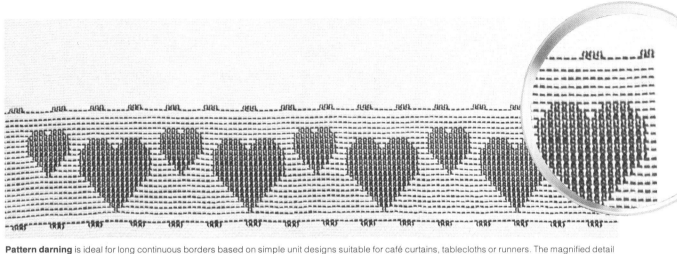

Pattern darning is ideal for long continuous borders based on simple unit designs suitable for café curtains, tablecloths or runners. The magnified detail shows the combination of closed loops and straight stitches.

Four basic motifs

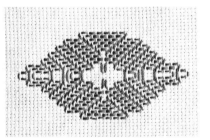

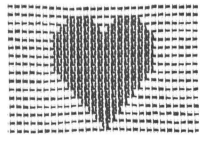

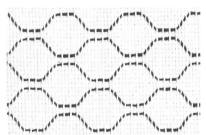

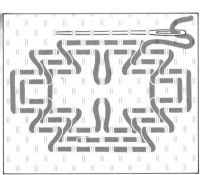

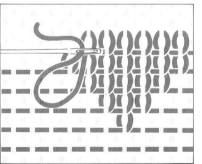

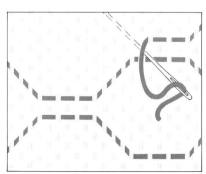

Single motif is worked from centre out. Design above consists of straight stitches, offsets and open loops.

Border is worked from bottom upwards in rows from right to left. Stitches used are straight stitches and figure-eights.

Stylised figure is worked from right to left in rows. The heart shape above is worked in rows of closed loops and straight stitches.

All-over pattern is worked in rows from right to left until desired area is filled. Pattern above is worked entirely in straight stitch.

For detailed stitch instructions, see next page.

Pattern darning

Basic stitch movements

Straight stitches are the type used most often in pattern darning. To work, move needle from right to left, picking up warp threads in a straight line. Needle can also move diagonally.

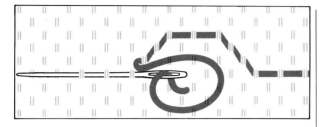

Offsets are darning stitches that create a stairway effect. To work, always move needle from right to left, and forwards.

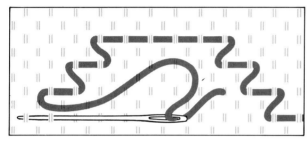

Open loops are darning stitches that are looped at the top and open at the base. Move needle from right to left, and forwards at each pick-up point, to keep the loops open.

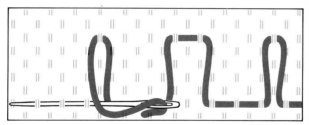

Closed loops are like open loops, but the stitch base is closed. To work, move needle from right to left at the base and from left to right at the top. *Re-enter under same thread* at base, moving right to left.

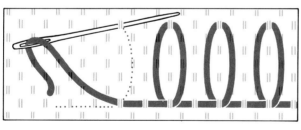

Figure-eights are a combination of open and closed loops. Move from right to left at base, and at top of loop. Figure-eight is formed by *re-entering under same warp thread on base line* to complete the stitch.

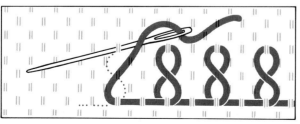

Working pattern darning

Most darning designs are worked in rows of stitches that start at the bottom and are built upwards. The first row of a design, however, is worked from the centre out to make sure the design is balanced on both sides. After this line is laid, rows can be worked from right to left. Many darning patterns consist of large motifs that are repeated. In order to fit as many full motifs as possible within the width of the fabric, the initial motif must be carefully placed.

To determine position of the first motif in relation to the centre of the fabric, count the number of warp threads that are spanned by one motif, then the number across the fabric. Divide the number of warp threads per motif into the number available in the fabric. Drop all fractions from the result. If the answer is an even number, place the edge of a motif on the centre line and work a complete motif on either side. If the answer is an odd number of floats, centre the first motif – that is, work half a motif on either side.

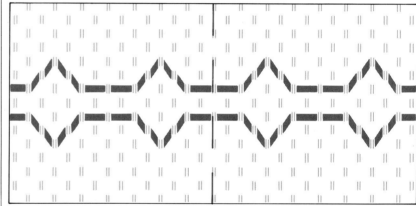

For an even number of darned motifs, start with two motifs, one on either side of the centre line of the fabric.

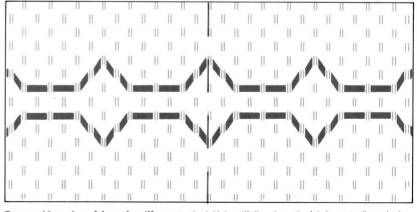

For an odd number of darned motifs, centre the initial motif directly on the fabric centre line, placing half on either side.

To start, fold fabric width in half; mark fold. Cut thread to suitable length (for one row across fabric without a join). Do not knot thread end. Leaving half of thread length free at centre, work first row from centre to left.

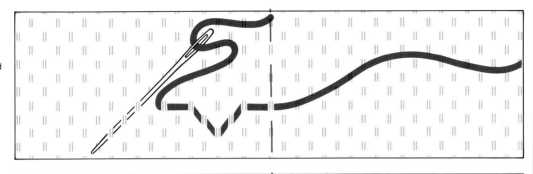

Turn work upside-down. Thread needle with free thread and work the other half of the row from the right to the left.

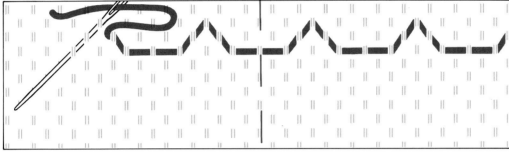

Turn work right side up again and work next row, going from right to left, using a continuous length of thread.

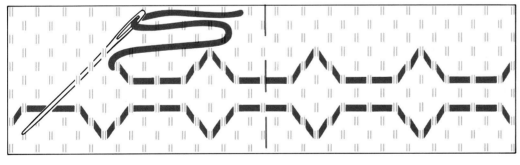

Work all other rows from right to left, using continuous lengths of thread. Stitch carefully, using the laid rows as a guide.

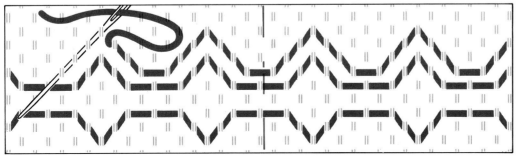

Finishing ends

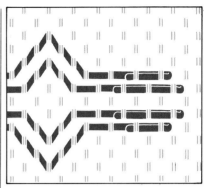

If a design is complete within an open area, weave thread ends back into final stitches.

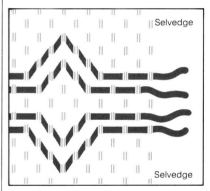

If a design runs all the way to a seam, leave ends free; they will be caught in seam.

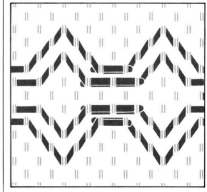

To join thread ends within pattern, run thread to very end. Start new thread 2.5 cm back.

Openwork/ Pulled thread embroidery

Introduction to pulled thread work
Working a pulled thread work piece
Stitch patterns

Introduction

Pulled thread embroidery (or drawn fabric work) is a type of openwork often employed to decorate linens. In pulled thread work, each stitch pulls the fabric threads together, creating open, lace-like patterns. Simple embroidery stitches are used also to outline motifs or to add textural interest.

Being a form of counted-thread embroidery, pulled thread work is usually stitched on even-weave fabrics. Select a thread similar in weight to a single fabric thread drawn from the fabric. Use the largest tapestry needle that will slip easily between fabric threads. This will exaggerate the openings. Use an embroidery hoop or frame, but do not stretch fabric too tightly or the stitches will not 'pull' effectively.

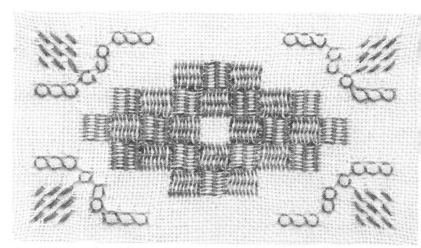

Pulled thread work piece combining three stitch patterns from the selection illustrated.

Working a pulled thread work piece

For any pulled thread work piece, first find the fabric centre and mark with tacking. Then position motifs, counting threads from centre point out. If outer edges of motif will be covered with an embroidery stitch, you can *draw* the outline on right side of fabric. If outline will not be covered, use tacking stitches. Work motifs one at a time, from centre one out; work stitch patterns in rows (see next three pages). Always secure row ends as shown below. Work all patterns, then add embellishments.

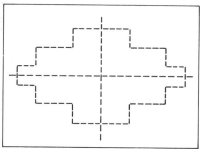

Mark centre of fabric, then draw or tack motifs on fabric, counting threads from centre.

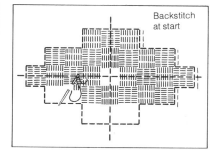

Work motif groups one at a time, from centre of piece out; work stitch patterns in rows.

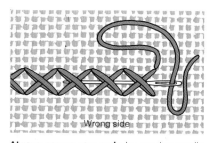

Always secure row ends by passing needle under worked stitches on wrong side. Then pull out the backstitches worked at the beginning and secure those thread ends the same way.

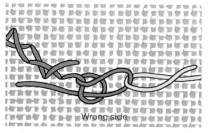

To tie in new thread. Make loop for simple knot; hold twisted part with thumbnail close to last stitch; pull to small circle; insert thread end to form second loop. Thread new thread; pull

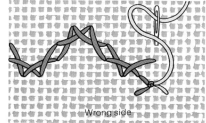

through second loop. With nail holding first knot, tug on second loop to pull first partly closed. Pull old and new threads opposite ways until second loop disappears and clicks through first. Trim.

Stitch patterns

Pulled thread embroidery offers quite a choice of stitch patterns. Here and on the next two pages we show step-by-step instructions for six of the most popular. Each stitch pattern is worked in rows.

Depending on the pattern, rows may run from side to side, horizontally or vertically. The needle movements are simple, though changing rows can be confusing. Follow each sequence carefully, noting the needle movements and direction in which the fabric is held. (Often it is turned for easier handling.) The last illustration in each sequence shows the look of the pulled threads.

Begin with a few backstitches outside the area to be worked. End by weaving thread into back of work. Finally, pull out the first backstitches and weave those, too, into the back of the work.

Four-sided stitch is worked in horizontal rows, always moving from right to left. To start, come up at 1, go in at 2 and out at 3 to the left of 1. Go in at 1 and come up at 4 above 3. Go in at 2, come up at 3. Pull each stitch tight. *Repeat sequence* until row is complete. For next row, turn fabric upside-down and work second row as you did first. At end of row, turn fabric again for start of third row.

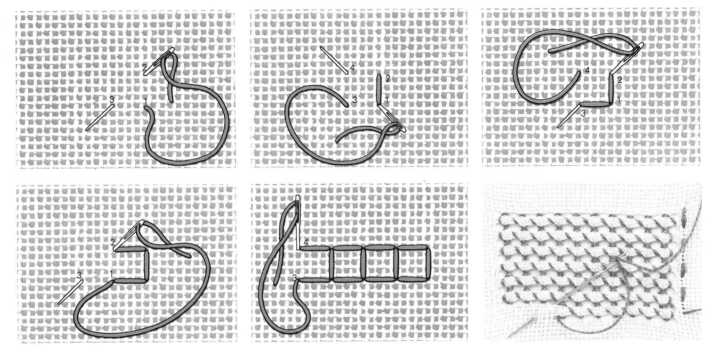

Coil filling stitch is made of groups of satin stitches worked in horizontal rows. To start, come up at 1 and work three satin stitches. Move to next group, four fabric threads to left, repeat Steps 1 to 6. At end of row, come up at 1 below for start of next row. Work second row left to right, third right to left.

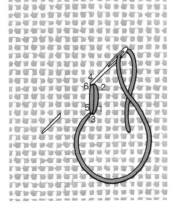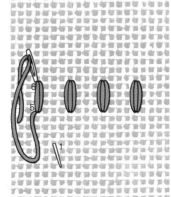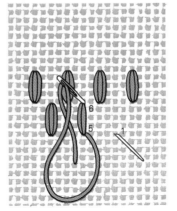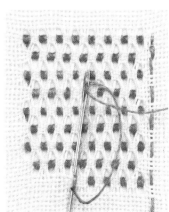

Openwork/Pulled thread embroidery

Stitch patterns

Chessboard filling stitch is worked in blocks. Each block is worked in three rows (eight stitches each) alternately right to left, then left to right. At end of third row, turn as shown and come up at 1 to start new block. *Work all subsequent blocks* like the first, turning as shown for each new block.

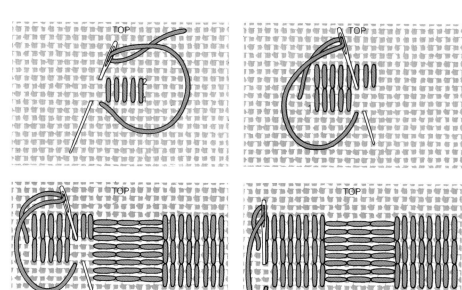

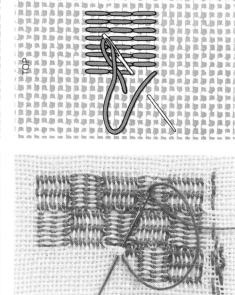

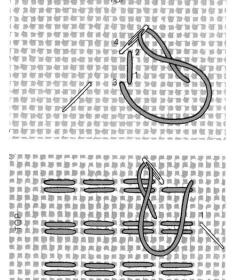

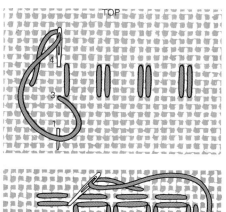

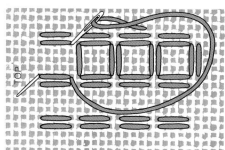

Framed cross is worked in two parts. First work the vertical pairs of stitches in rows alternately from right to left, then left to right, until desired number of rows are completed. *Then turn fabric* as shown and work pairs of stitches perpendicular to the first set, working rows alternately right to left, then left to right.

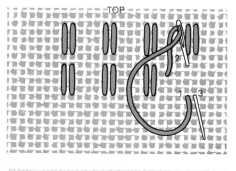

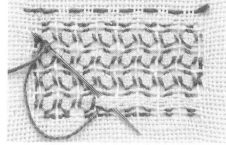

74

Ringed backstitch is worked in two journeys. In the first, a series of half-rings are formed. In the second journey, the rings are completed. To start, come up at 1, go in at 2 and out at 3. Continue working backstitches through Step 9. (A 1 to 9 sequence forms two half-rings or eight stitches.) *Repeat sequence* until desired number of half-rings are formed. At end of row, turn fabric and work other half of rings as shown. Always move from right to left; turn fabric to accomplish this.

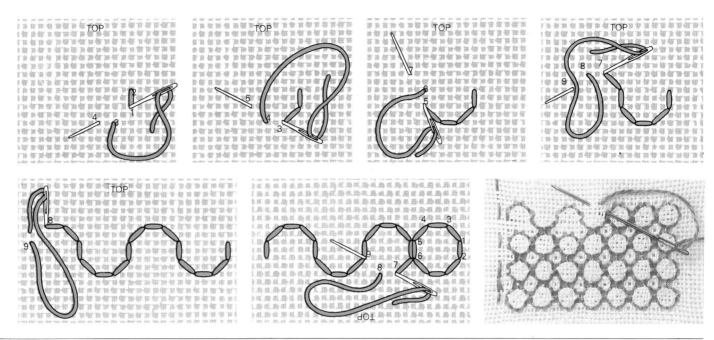

Reverse faggot stitch is worked in pairs of diagonal rows. Worked as shown, stitch fills a square area. Square is worked one half at a time. To start, come up at 1, go in at 2 and out at 3 directly across from 2. Go in at 4, come up at 2. Repeat the sequence until two rows are formed, having four and three stitches respectively. (Subsequent rows shorten similarly to form a corner of the square.) Turn fabric to begin next rows. *Using same 1 to 4 sequence,* work second pair of rows. Turn fabric upright for third pair. Work the other half of the square the same way. Note that because the second set of rows uses some of the same holes as the first set, double lines of stitching are formed.

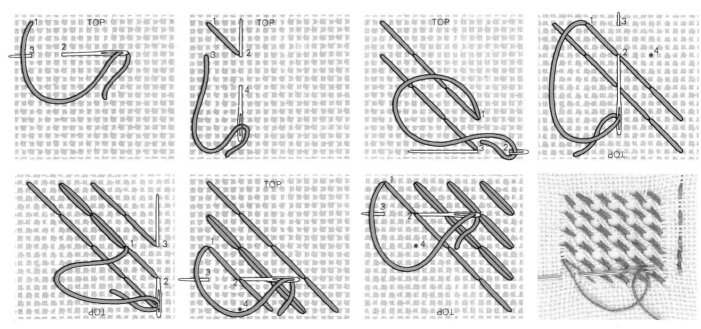

Openwork/ Drawn thread work

Drawn thread work techniques

Drawn thread work is a type of openwork embroidery in which some of the weft and warp threads are drawn out or removed from the fabric. The remaining threads in the drawn area are then grouped together by means of different stitches, creating an open, lacy effect. There are two basic types of drawn thread work, **hemstitching** and **needleweaving**, both used primarily for border decorations on table linen. Fabric threads are drawn out the same way in both hemstitching and needleweaving. They differ in the way the remaining threads are decorated.

Introduction to hemstitching

Hemstitching is the most common type of drawn thread work. It is called hemstitching because as it groups threads within a drawn border, it may also hem the edge below the border. It can also be used solely to group threads in a drawn border, without a hemmed edge.

Almost any woven fabric can be used, though an even-weave is easiest to handle. Select a thread of a thickness comparable to one strand of your fabric. Use stranded cotton or fine pearl cotton and work with a tapestry needle.

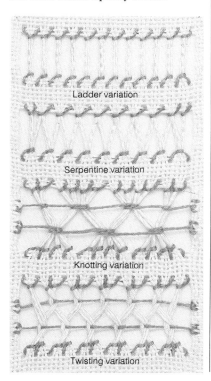

Ladder variation

Serpentine variation

Knotting variation

Twisting variation

Preparing fabric for hemstitching

To prepare an edge for hemstitching, you must first decide how deep and wide the border will be. Exact width and depth depend on the stitch variation you select (see pp. 78–79). Each one calls for the grouping of a certain number of vertical threads; a border's actual width will be a multiple of the threads in one group. Stitch variations differ, too, in depth, as the illustrations show.

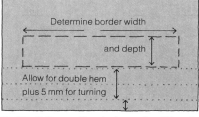

Decide distance of border from edge. If hem is needed, allow twice hem depth plus 5 mm for turning. Tack mark as explained below.

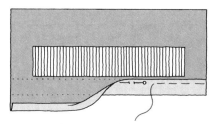

After drawing threads, press raw edge under; press hem up so top edge is one fabric thread from bottom of border. Pin and tack hem.

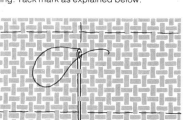

Drawing threads. 1. Tack along top and bottom of border between two horizontal threads. Tack-mark approximate width, then the centre.

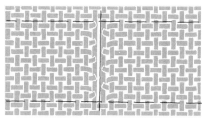

2. Using a pair of sharp embroidery scissors, carefully cut the horizontal fabric threads at the centre of the marked border.

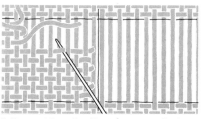

3. Draw out threads with a tapestry needle, leaving free the exact number of vertical threads for the stitch variation you plan to work.

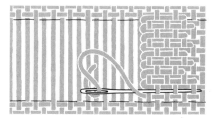

4. At border edges, weave fabric threads back into the wrong side of the fabric for 2.5 cm. Trim excess after weaving.

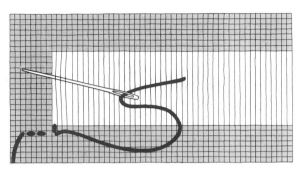

Without a hem, basic hemstitch is usually worked from wrong side of fabric. To start, leave 15 cm of thread and work backstitches up to left edge of border. Take a small vertical stitch to right of edge. Then pass needle from right to left under fixed number (3-5) of vertical threads. Pull together into bundle.

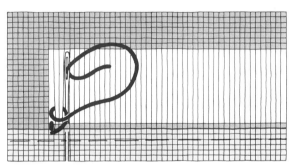

With a hem, too, basic hemstitch is usually worked from wrong side. To start, bring needle up at left edge of border, securing thread in hem fold with a simple knot. Take small vertical stitch just to right of edge, being sure to catch hem. Then pass needle under fixed number of vertical threads (3-5) and pull together into bundle.

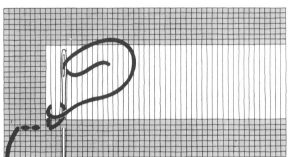

Take a small vertical stitch under two horizontal threads to the right of the bundle. Continue working in this way over the entire width of the border, keeping the small vertical stitches even throughout.

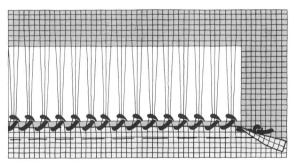

Take a small vertical stitch through right side, emerging at hem fold, to right of thread bundle. Continue working in this way across entire width of border.

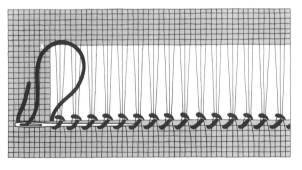

At end of border, still on the wrong (working) side, pass needle through completed stitches to secure. Pull out the backstitches at left edge of border and secure these as well by passing the thread through the completed stitches there.

When the stitching is complete, secure it by passing needle through hem fold and hem stitches. Trim excess thread.

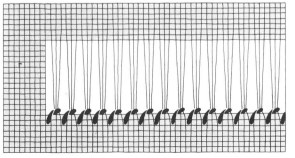

The finished effect on the right side (when work is done on the wrong side) is shown on the left. If you prefer the look of the small loops formed on the working side, as shown immediately above, work hemstitching from right side of fabric. Secure thread ends on the wrong side; they should, of course, be invisible.

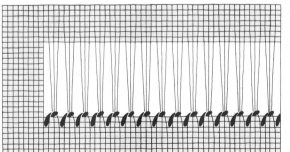

Look of right side (when worked from the wrong) is shown on the left. If you prefer the looped effect shown above, work hemstitching from the right side of the fabric, being sure to catch hem, which will not be visible as you work. Finish off thread ends, of course, on the wrong side.

Openwork/Drawn thread work

Grouping variations

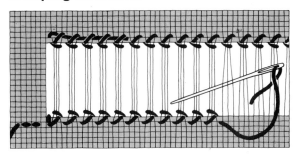

Ladder variation. To work, complete a row of basic hemstitch. Turn work upside-down and work basic stitch on opposite edge. Stitch from left to right, catching the same threads in each bundle as were caught above to form a ladder-like pattern. Secure thread at both ends as for basic hemstitch.

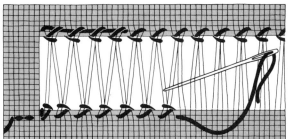

Serpentine variation. To work, complete a row of basic hemstitch, making sure each bundle has an *even* number of threads. Turn and work basic stitch on other edge, grouping halves of adjacent bundles together. First and last bundles will contain half as many threads as other bundles.

Knotting variations

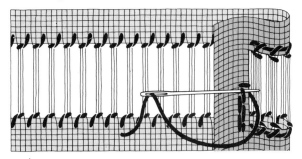

Simple knotted effect. To work, begin with a ladder variation on a border at least 1 cm deep. (Number of bundles must be a multiple of number grouped in second step.) Secure thread by working backstitches along right edge of border. Then oversew as shown, emerging at centre, from wrong side, for next step.

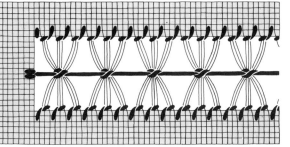

Continue working over remaining groups of bundles. When border is complete, oversew at left edge to fasten, then weave end of thread invisibly into back of fabric. Pull out the backstitches at opposite end and secure them the same way.

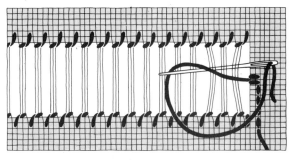

Working from right side of fabric, group the desired number of bundles (here three) as follows: loop thread as shown; pass needle behind thread and under bundles; bring needle out with thread under point.

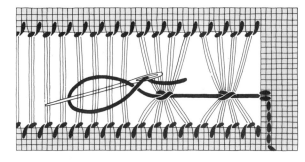

Double knotted effect. To work, draw out border at least 1.5 cm deep. Work a ladder variation. (The number of ladder bundles must be a multiple of 4.) Then work a simple knot, grouping four bundles one-third of the way up the drawn border.

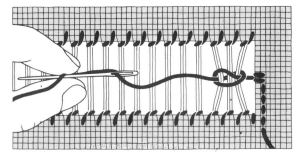

Pull needle through to form knot around bundles at the centre of the border depth. This is a version of coral stitch (p. 29).

Work the same knot two-thirds of the way up the border, taking adjacent halves of the bottom bundles in each knot. The first and last groups will contain half as many bundles as the others.

Twisting variations

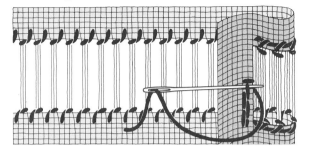

Simple twisted border. To work, complete ladder variation on a border at least 1 cm deep. (Work an even number of bundles.) Then, on right side of fabric, secure end of thread by backstitching along the right edge. Oversew as shown, emerging at centre, from wrong side, for next step.

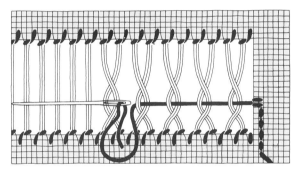

Multiple bundles can be twisted in the same way that two are twisted. (For the variation shown here, number of bundles must be a multiple of 4.)

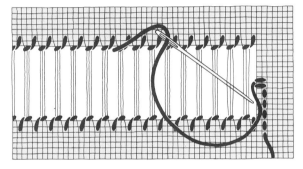

Working from right side of fabric, place needle over first two bundles. Then angle it down and towards the right, going under the second bundle and over the first with the tip of the needle.

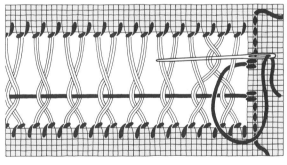

Double twisted effect. Draw out a border at least 1.5 cm deep and work a ladder variation. (The number of bundles must be a multiple of 2.) Then work a simple twisting stitch one-third of the way up, grouping two bundles together.

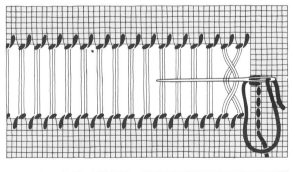

Press tip of needle against the first bundle and scoop it to the left, under the second bundle. Pulling the first bundle under the second causes the two to cross as shown.

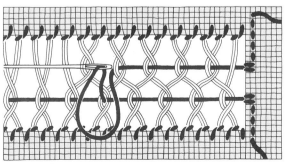

Work the same simple twisting stitch at the top one-third of the border, but go under the first bundle before beginning actual twisting. The first bundle is missed in order to stagger twisting points of the top and bottom rows.

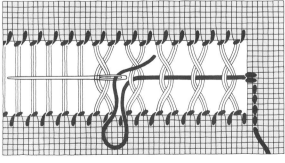

Pull the needle through, keeping thread taut to hold bundles in position. Continue working over pairs of bundles until entire border is twisted. At left edge, fasten thread with oversewing, then weave end invisibly into back of fabric. Remove backstitches at opposite end; secure the same way.

Continue twisting in this way until border is completed. Be sure to keep thread taut to hold intricate pattern in place. Fasten end of thread on left edge of border with oversewing. Weave end invisibly into back of fabric. Remove backstitches at opposite end and secure them in the same way.

Openwork/Drawn thread work

Handling drawn corners

Often a drawn thread border of hemstitching (or of needleweaving) will run along all four edges of an article such as a napkin, a tablecloth or a handkerchief. This will result in completely open corner areas where both warp and weft fabric threads have been drawn out. Drawn corners, depending on their size, can either be left open or decoratively filled with additional stitches. A small corner can be left open. A larger one should be filled to give it stability.

Decorating drawn corners

When the hemstitched border is shallow (less than 1.5 cm), the open corners will be small and can be left open. The outer edges of the corner, however, should be reinforced with the **basic buttonhole stitch** or **tailor's buttonhole stitch**.

When the border is deep (1.5 cm or more), the corners will be larger. These should be reinforced with a buttonhole stitch, then decorated as well. Decora-tive stitches help to strengthen large corners. Two such stitches are shown on these pages, **loopstitch** and **dove's eye filling**. Loopstitch forms a simple, flower-like motif and can be used with basic hemstitch or any hemstitch variation that has a straight bundle at each corner edge. Dove's eye filling forms an 'X' with a circular centre and can be used with any form of hemstitching.

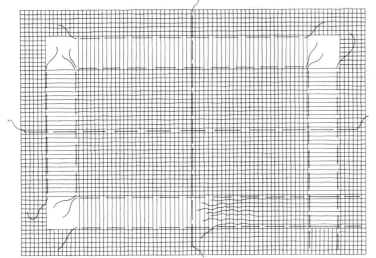

To prepare for corners, cut fabric to desired size, including hem allowance (see p. 76). Tack through horizontal and vertical centres. Measure and tack border's outer edges, then its inner edges; keep tackings between fabric threads. Draw threads (p. 76), being sure that all sides contain the correct number for the stitch variation chosen. Hem as described at far right on opposite page.

BUTTONHOLE STITCHES

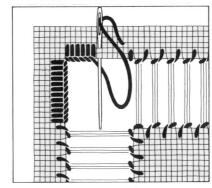

Basic buttonhole stitch. Work on outer edges of all corners, whether to be open or filled. Stitch from right side, two to three fabric threads deep, catching hem if there is one.

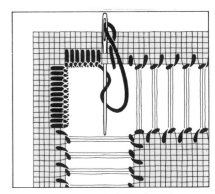

Tailor's buttonhole stitch. An alternative to the basic buttonhole stitch, and worked like it except that the thread is wrapped around the needle as shown before it is pulled through.

Hemstitching to and around corners

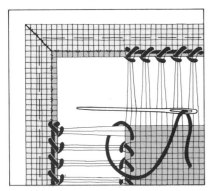

Hemstitch outer edges first, ending with small vertical stitch at last bundle of threads. To secure, pass thread through completed stitches; secure other end the same way, removing backstitches.

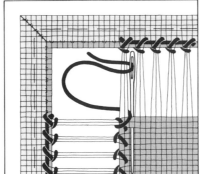

Hemstitching at the **inner edges** turns corners. Notice that thread simply wraps the last bundle on the left edge, then the first one on the top edge, before the small vertical stitch is taken.

DOVE'S EYE FILLING

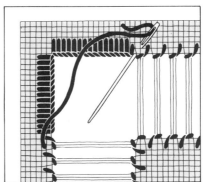

Dove's eye. 1. First reinforce edges with buttonhole stitch. Then bring needle up at lower left corner. Insert needle in fabric at upper right corner, coming out at corner opening.

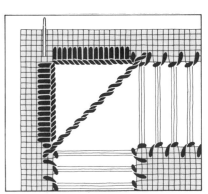

2. Oversew the laid thread, working from upper right to lower left corner. Take needle to back of fabric and slip it through the buttonhole stitches, coming up at top left corner of square.

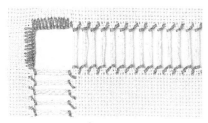

Buttonhole stitch reinforcing corner edges.

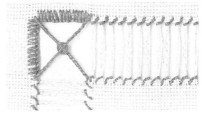

Loopstitch worked in large open corner.

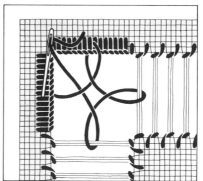

Dove's eye worked in large open corner.

Hemming corners

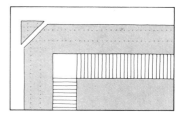

To hem corners, press under 5 mm on raw edges. Press hem so fold is just below border edge. Unfold pressed hem.

LOOPSTITCH

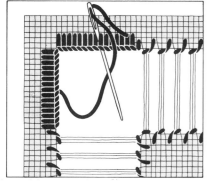

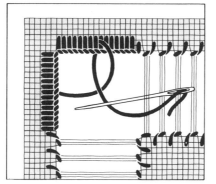

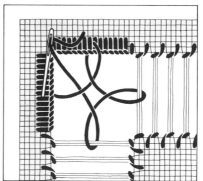

Loopstitch. 1. Work buttonhole stitch on outer edges. Then draw thread through underside of stitches, coming up at left centre. Take a stitch at top centre (thread passes under needle).

2. Loop needle over and under bundle at right edge; keep thread under needle. Do not pull thread too tightly; leave some slack to create open-looking loops and to avoid distortion.

3. Loop needle over and under bundle at bottom edge. Pass needle under thread at left edge and take a stitch at left centre. Run needle through buttonhole stitches on wrong side to secure.

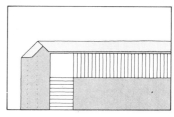

Trim off each corner diagonally as shown above, cutting along the diagonal of the corner square formed by the creases.

DOVE'S EYE FILLING–continued

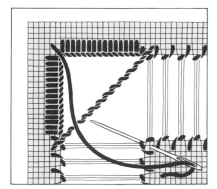

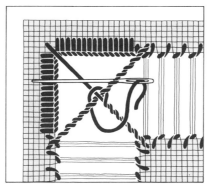

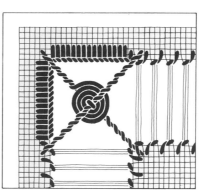

3. Bring needle over laid thread and insert into fabric at lower right corner. Come out again at the opening, pulling the thread tight enough to form an even 'X' with the other laid thread.

4. Oversew second laid thread to the point where the two threads cross. Weave under and over the laid threads at centre point, going anti-clockwise, until dove's eye is desired size.

5. Oversew remainder of diagonal yarn to upper left corner. Secure stitching thread at back of fabric by running needle through buttonhole stitches along top edge of open square.

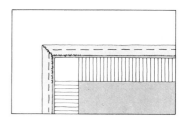

Turn down trimmed corner first. Then re-fold hem edges along the pressed lines to form neat, mitred corners.

Pin and tack hem. Slipstitch mitred edges, also tack hem edge along outer corner. Hemstitch hem in place (p. 77).

Openwork/Drawn thread work

Needleweaving

Needleweaving, like hemstitching, decorates threads in a drawn thread border. In needleweaving, however, thread bundles are covered, with the thread ends secured under the covering.

The basic stitches are *overcast stitch* and *darning stitch*. Overcasting wraps the drawn threads, forming vertical bars. Darning weaves over and under them, giving a braid-like finish.

If needleweaving is 'attached' (covers the bundles), the border is not usually hemstitched. (The hem, if there is one, must then be slipstitched.) Hemstitching is advised for 'detached' types (see darning variation on opposite page).

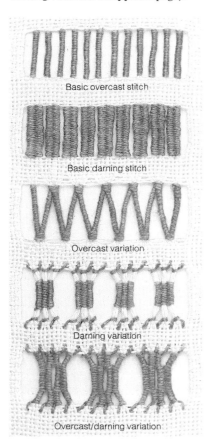

Basic overcast stitch

Basic darning stitch

Overcast variation

Darning variation

Overcast/darning variation

Basic needleweaving stitches

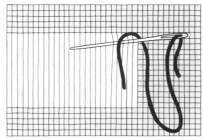

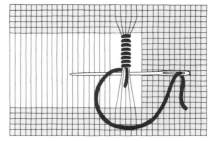

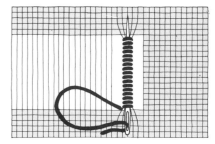

Basic overcast stitch. Place end of working thread over the five threads to be overcast. Wrap working thread over threads and thread end.

Pull threads taut as you work. Place them close together with the needle from time to time. Take care not to let wrapping threads overlap.

When bar is completed, run needle through it to secure thread. If fit is tight, change to a thinner, sharp-pointed needle. Trim excess thread.

Needleweaving variations

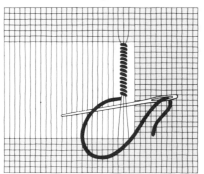

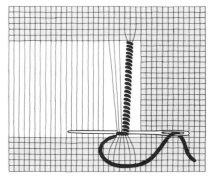

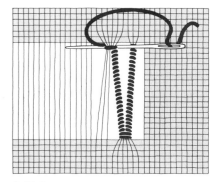

Overcast variation. Prepare drawn border, with total threads a multiple of three. **1.** Work one basic overcast bar over three threads.

2. Just above bottom edge of border, overcast twice over six threads as shown, pulling first and second bundles together.

3. Work up over second three-thread bundle. At top, overcast twice over six threads, pulling second and third bundles together.

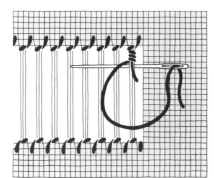

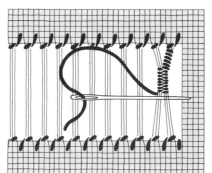

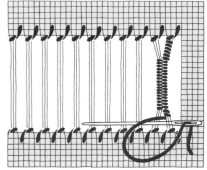

Overcast/darning variation. Bundles multiple of four, three threads each in ladder hemstitch. **1.** Overcast top quarter of first bundle.

2. Change to darning stitch and darn over and under first and second groups of threads until three-quarters of the border depth is covered.

3. Change back to overcasting stitch and wrap the remainder of the first group of threads to the bottom edge of the border.

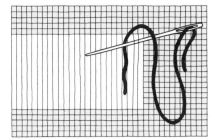

Basic darning stitch. Lay thread end along first four threads. Pass needle under first two (have thread behind needle); pull it through. Then pass

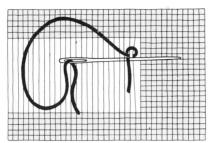

needle back under second two threads, grouping four threads and thread end together, in figure-eight movement. Continue weaving

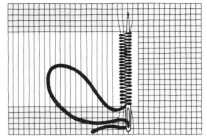

needle over and back until bar is covered. To secure thread, run needle through woven bar; if fit is tight, change to thinner needle. Trim.

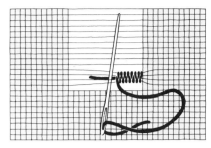

If working across vertical bars is awkward for you, **turn the work** so that the bar lies **horizontally,** and work darning stitch as shown.

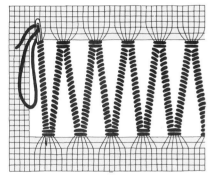

4. Continue this way to end of border, creating a zigzag effect. Run needle through last bar to secure yarn; change to thinner needle if fit is tight.

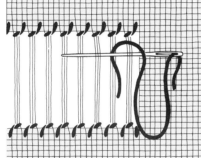

Darning variation. Work ladder hemstitch (see p. 78), with ladder bundles a multiple of 3. **1.** To begin, place needle as shown above.

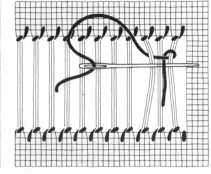

2. Darn three bundles together along centre half, moving needle right to left, left to right until centre half is darned. Pull thread taut as you weave.

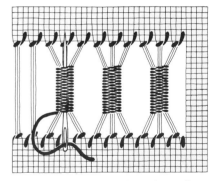

3. As each bar is completed, run the needle up through it to secure thread; trim excess. If fit is tight, change to a thinner needle.

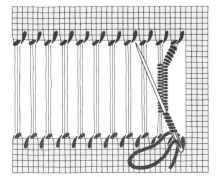

4. Slip needle up through these last overcasting stitches to get into position for next step. If fit is tight, change to thinner needle.

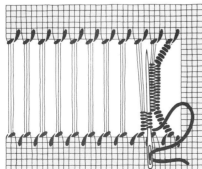

5. Darn second and third groups together to bottom edge. Run thread through just-darned area; use thinner needle if necessary. Trim.

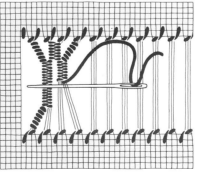

6. Turn work upside-down and, using new length of thread, repeat entire sequence to fill in other half of pattern. Turn right side up for next one.

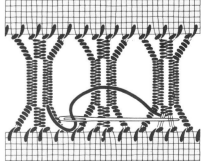

7. Continue working individual units by halves, the first half right side up, the work turned for second half, until border is filled.

Openwork/ Hardanger embroidery

Introduction to Hardanger
Kloster blocks
Working a motif
Covered bars
Filling stitches
Decorating a motif

Introduction

Hardanger embroidery is a type of openwork named after the district of Hardanger in Norway. Similar work was done in Persia centuries ago.

Hardanger is characterised by precisely worked blocks of satin stitch called **kloster blocks.** These are arranged to form the outer shapes of motifs and are often worked within these shapes as well. When blocks have been stitched, warp and weft threads are cut and drawn out in appropriate places (where there are kloster blocks opposite each other to secure ends). Remaining fabric threads within the motifs are covered to form either **overcast** or **woven bars.** The open squares between bars can be decorated with various filling stitches. Often surface stitching is added to enhance the overall design.

Because Hardanger is a type of counted thread embroidery, it is advisable to plot a piece on graph paper – first the shapes and placings of motifs, then bars, fillings and embellishments. To prepare the piece for working, tack the outline of each motif on the fabric.

The work is generally done on Hardanger fabric, which has double warp and weft threads. Almost any evenweave fabric will do, however. Because kloster blocks are worked over a uniform number of fabric threads, the finer the fabric (the more threads per centimetre), the smaller a motif will be.

Ideally, two sizes of thread are used. Thread for kloster blocks should be slightly thicker than the threads of the fabric; the usual choice is a medium-weight pearl cotton. To cover bars and work filling stitches, thread should be thinner – either a fine pearl cotton or a suitable number of stranded cotton strands. Originally, Hardanger was worked with white thread on white fabric; today both thread and fabric are often coloured.

Always do this work in an embroidery hoop or frame.

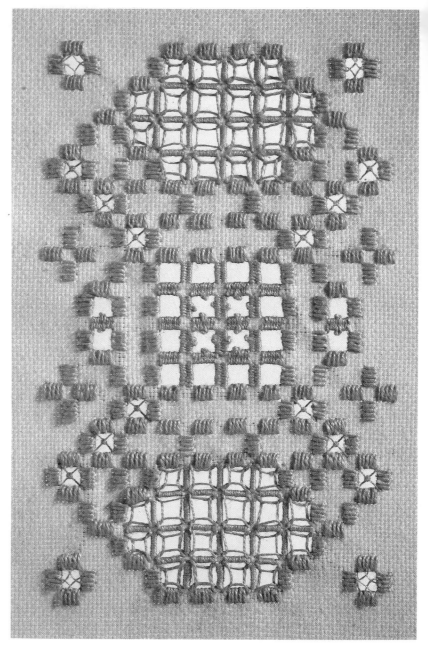

Hardanger piece of overcast bars, woven bars, loopstitches and dove's eyes (pp. 86–87)

84

Kloster blocks

The basic kloster block consists of five satin stitches worked over four fabric threads. In a motif, the blocks may be worked across in rows or diagonally in steps. In placing the blocks, remember that they must be opposite each other where warp and weft threads will be cut. While the basic kloster block is always worked in the same way, the movement from block to block varies with the arrangement. When blocks are in steps (see drawings below), stitching direction alternates from row to row.

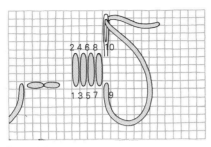

To work kloster block, secure thread end with backstitches; come up at 1 and work five satin stitches, each over four fabric threads.

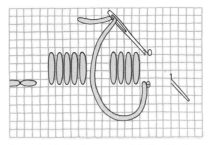

To work blocks in a row, stitch first block as usual. At end, come up four fabric threads to the right of point 9 to start the next block.

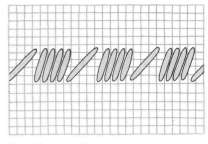

When kloster blocks are worked in a row, there should be single slanting threads from block to block on the **wrong side** of the fabric.

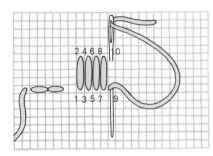

To work blocks diagonally in steps, stitch first block as usual. At the end, come up again at point 9 where the last satin stitch began.

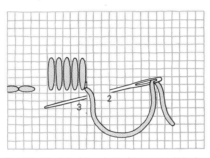

Point 9 of first block is point 1 of the second block. Start the second block by working a *horizontal* satin stitch over four fabric threads.

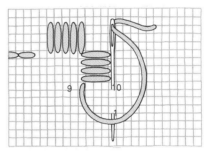

Work last stitch of second block as usual (up at 9, in at 10). Come up four fabric threads below 10 to start *vertical* stitches of third block.

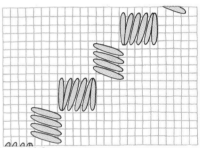

When kloster blocks are worked diagonally, there should be no trailing threads between blocks on the **wrong side** of the fabric.

Working a motif

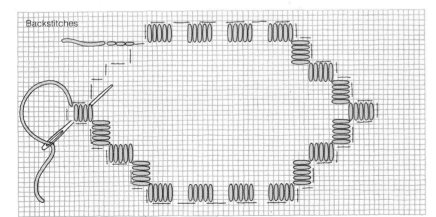

To work a motif. Tack shape on to fabric. Secure thread end with backstitches. Working clockwise, go from block to block as instructed above. For every block where threads will be cut, another must be worked directly opposite, in the same direction, enclosing the same fabric threads. At end of motif, run thread under five blocks to secure. Pull out backstitches and secure thread the same way.

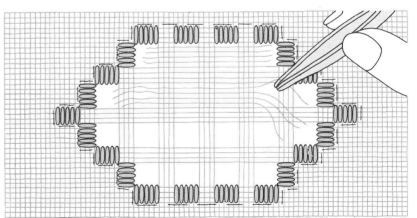

To remove threads. With sharp embroidery scissors, cut four threads at the base of a kloster block; cut *same* four threads at base of opposing block. (All cut threads must be secured at both ends by blocks.) Cut only threads that run the same way as satin stitches – never those the satin stitches cross. Remove threads with tweezers. Draw all appropriate threads running one way, then those running the other.

Openwork/Hardanger embroidery

Covered bars

When kloster blocks have been worked and threads drawn, motifs are usually decorated. The loose threads are **overcast** or **woven** into covered bars; *picots* (loops) can be added to woven bars during weaving. Open areas are generally embellished with filling stitches. Secure beginning thread with backstitches. To start a new thread, secure thread end under next bar as you cover it.

Filling stitches

The three filling stitches shown in the sampler on the right and explained below are **oblique loopstitch, straight loopstitch** and **dove's eye filling.** These are basic filling techniques that, like other aspects of Hardanger embroidery, can be and are varied in many ways.

Fillings differ, too, in their usage. They can be worked to fill all the open areas in a motif, as suggested in the illustrations on the far right. Or squares can be filled selectively. An area can be filled with one kind of stitch, or several.

The directional and other advice given earlier applies equally to the working of filling stitches. The recommendation that bars and fillings be worked diagonally is simply for convenience; it is generally easier to pass from bar to bar in this direction. If an area is to be worked in bars alone, many needleworkers recommend working all bars in one direction, then all bars in the other.

When all work on a motif is finished, run the thread through the backs of five or more kloster blocks to secure it; remove the beginning backstitches and secure them the same way. Start a new thread by working over its beginning end as you cover the next bar. For details of this manoeuvre, and some other useful similarities between Hardanger embroidery and needleweaving, refer to pp. 82–83.

Overcast bars   **Woven bars**   **Woven bars with picots**

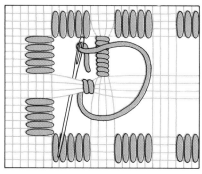
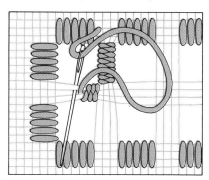
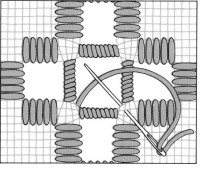
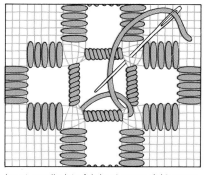

To overcast a bar, wrap thread compactly around thread bundle; to weave a bar, bring needle up in centre of bundle and weave thread over and under pairs of threads. As bundles are covered, move in diagonal steps from bar to bar, passing thread behind threads or through backs of kloster blocks.

Oblique loopstitch. Come up at lower left, go in at lower right, come up at opening. With thread under needle, pull it through, leaving a loop.

Insert needle into fabric at upper right corner, come up at opening. Making sure thread is under needle, pull it through, again leaving a loop.

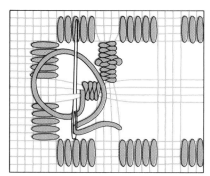
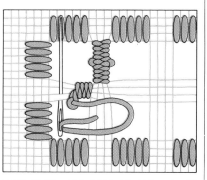
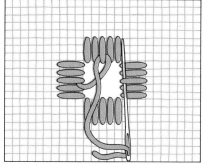
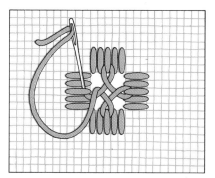

Woven bar with picot. Weave half of bar. Bring needle up through centre; loop thread under it as shown. Pull thread through to form small loop.

Insert needle under same two threads and pull it through. Work another picot through two threads on opposite side. Weave rest of bar.

Straight loopstitch in area enclosed by kloster blocks. Come up at left below centre stitch; loop thread right to left through top centre stitch.

Continue working around square, looping thread through centre stitch at each side. Always carry thread under needle. Stitch last loop as shown.

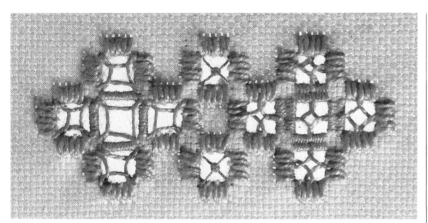

Filling stitches shown are, left to right, **oblique loopstitch, dove's eye** and **straight loopstitch.**

Decorating a motif

Because Hardanger designs vary so widely, it is difficult to give precise rules to suit all of them. It will help, however, especially on the first try, to understand some general principles that can be applied to most typical motifs. With those, and some practical experience, it should not be long before you can work Hardanger embroidery with the traditional precision and delicacy.

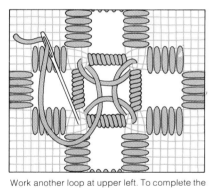

Work another loop at upper left. To complete the stitch, pass needle under first laid thread and insert it into fabric at lower left corner.

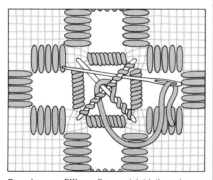

Dove's eye filling. Crossed laid threads are woven over and under at centre to form circular filling. For instructions, see pp. 80–81.

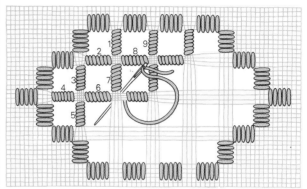

To work bars, most experts recommend the procedure shown, which progresses in diagonal steps from the upper left over four bars (1-4), then up in similar steps over five bars (5-9), and so on until all thread bundles are covered. Bars can be worked in two journeys: first all bars across, then, with work turned, all bars in the other direction.

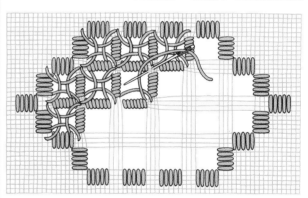

Oblique loops worked with bars go in the same general direction, the thread being passed behind adjacent fabric threads to reach the next opening. It is important to pass the threads in such a way that they are hidden. To start a new thread when needed, secure it in the most convenient bar.

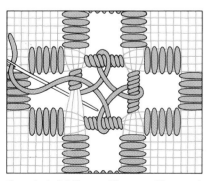

To work **straight loops with overcast bars,** work 3½ bars. Before working last half, make loops as on the left. Finish overcasting of last bar.

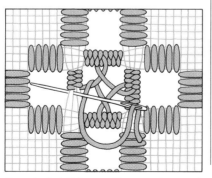

To work **straight loops with woven bars,** work 3½ bars. Then work loops, going through centre of bars (over two threads). Weave last half of bar.

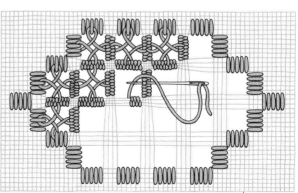

Straight loops with bars vary according to the sides of the opening that they are to fill – that is, whether individual loops go to a woven or overcast bar, or to a kloster block. The drawings on the left will refresh your memory.

Openwork/ Cutwork embroidery

Introduction to cutwork
Basic procedure
Making a cutwork piece

Introduction

Cutwork is a form of openwork embroidery that became fashionable in the 16th century and is still popular today, primarily for table linens and clothes. Despite its delicate look, cutwork is quite sturdy because each part of the design is outlined in close buttonhole stitch. After outlining, certain portions are cut away, giving the embroidery its characteristic airiness. Large cut-out areas are reinforced with embroidered bars, worked to bridge the areas and strengthen the work. Surface stitches are often added to enhance a cutwork design.

Closely woven fabrics (those not likely to fray) should be used for cutwork. Stitch with pearl cotton or stranded cotton and a sharp-pointed needle in a size that accommodates your thread. Use an embroidery hoop or frame while working the outline stitches. Remove work from frame before cutting.

Generally, the motifs in cutwork are floral, but other kinds can be used. In choosing a design, consider what areas will be cut away. If you are designing your own cutwork piece, think of the cut areas as negative and the uncut areas as positive, and try to balance the two.

There are three basic ways of arranging these positive and negative spaces. One is the stencil design, in which a motif is established by cutting away its main sections. (The small flowers in the sample are stencil designs.) Or a motif can be left intact and the background cut away, silhouetting the motif. (The stems and leaves in the sample are handled in this way.) Buttonhole-stitch outlining gives the shapes further definition. The third approach leaves some of the motif whole, with only small, interior sections cut away. This technique must be employed to achieve the shaped edge that is so attractive a feature of cutwork – it is the only one that permits a motif to be positioned at the very edge. (See the large corner flower in the sample.)

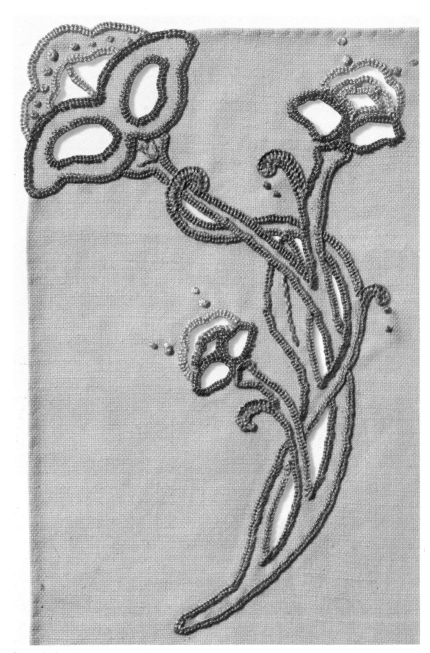

Cutwork piece features floral motifs. All outlining (in buttonhole stitch) is worked before cutting.

Basic procedure

The basic procedure for cutwork is quite simple, but the steps must be taken neatly and carefully to get professional results. The two main stitches in cutwork are **buttonhole stitch** and **running stitch**. The motifs are first 'drawn' with running stitches, then buttonhole stitch is worked over these lines. Be sure you know which side of a motif line will be cut away; the buttonhole stitch must be worked so that the ridge lies along the edge to be cut. If the fabric will be cut away on both sides of a line, outlining can be done with a **double buttonhole stitch** (two facing rows of the basic stitch, slightly overlapped at the centre).

To be sure that you will recognise the areas that are to be cut away, mark them before beginning to work the buttonhole stitch. On commercial transfers, open sections are often indicated by an 'X' that transfers on to the fabric. If you are creating your own design, you may wish to use a similar method.

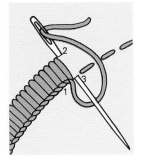

Buttonhole stitch is worked from left to right. Come up at 1, insert at 2, and come up at 3 directly below 2. Carry thread under needle point, pull through. Take care to keep stitches close together.
Double buttonhole stitch is two rows of the basic stitch. Work stitches in first row so that those of second row can go between them. Turn work to stitch second row.

Making a cutwork piece

First outline the design with *running stitches* (using either stranded cotton or pearl cotton). **Then cover the stitched shape** of the motif with a fine, close *buttonhole stitch*. Make certain that the ridge of the stitch falls on the side of the line that is to be cut away. Tailor's buttonhole stitch may also be used for this purpose. **Cut away design areas** indicated after removing work from frame or hoop. Work from the *wrong side;* this makes it easier to cut close to the base of the stitches. Be careful not to cut into the buttonhole stitches.

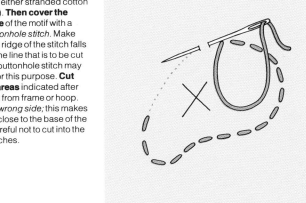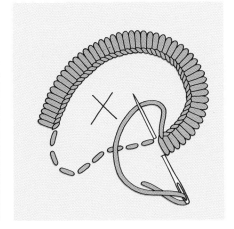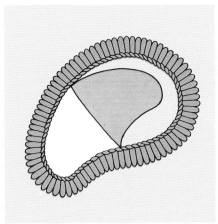

To work bars across an area, outline the design with running stitches until you come to a position for a bar. Carry thread across the area, take a small stitch, bring the thread back and take another stitch. **Work buttonhole stitch** over the laid thread *without catching fabric beneath*. Continue the running stitch around the rest of the motif, then outline it with fine buttonhole stitch. Cut away the fabric as above, taking care not to cut stitches.

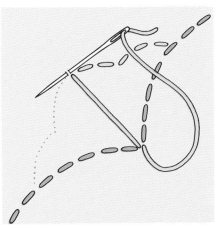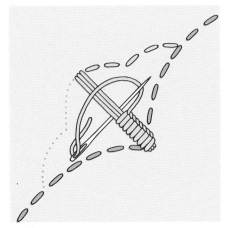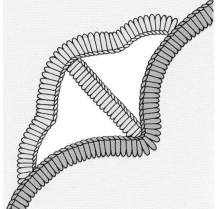

Smocking

Introduction

Smocking is a type of embroidery that decorates as well as gathers the fabric on which it is worked. It is based on a grid that is marked on the fabric in evenly spaced dots. Hot-iron transfers of smocking dots can be bought, or you can make your own dotted grid.

There are two basic smocking methods, **'mock' smocking** and **traditional.** In mock smocking, dots are marked on the *right* side of the fabric. The smocking stitches are worked from dot to dot, with the fabric gathered in each stitch. In traditional smocking, dots are marked on the *wrong* side of the fabric. Rows of uneven running stitches are worked from dot to dot, forming small, even pleats (known as 'tubes' or 'reeds'). Smocking stitches are then worked from the *right* side of the fabric, with a small stitch taken at each tube formed by the gathering. The look of the stitches is the same, regardless of the smocking method. The traditional method is particularly useful when combining different stitches (see p. 95).

Fabrics and grids

Smocking, as a rule, is worked on soft, lightweight fabrics (cotton, lawn, fine wool) with pearl cotton or stranded cotton and a crewel or chenille needle.

Since smocking gathers the fabric, you should work on a piece two and a half to three times the desired finished width. This proportion of flat to gathered width is approximate. How much is actually drawn up depends on fabric weight, stitch tension and the spacing between dots.

A smocking grid can be produced by

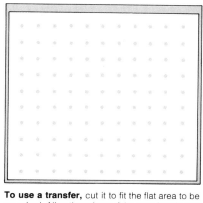

To use a transfer, cut it to fit the flat area to be smocked. Align the edges of the transfer with the fabric, leaving a seam allowance above the top row of dots. Press carefully.

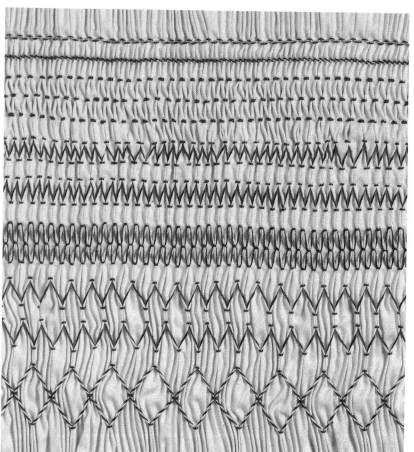

Smocking sampler of cable, stem, honeycomb, surface honeycomb, Vandyke, wave, trellis stitches.

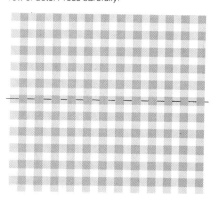

Even-weave fabrics, or even prints such as polka dots or gingham, need not be marked with transfer. The natural grid can guide your running stitches and gathering proceeds quickly.

means of a hot-iron transfer. You can also plan your own on graph paper, or use an even-weave or an evenly printed fabric as a guide. Space between dots is usually from 3 to 5 mm; between rows of dots, from 3 mm to 1 cm. The closer the dots, the more elasticity the finished smocking will have.

While most stitches can be worked on any smocking grid without their appearance being markedly altered, some stitches require grids of a specific proportion.

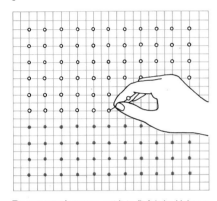

To use graph paper, cut it to fit fabric. Using a sharp stiletto or a needle or pin, pierce dots in paper to desired spacing. Place paper on fabric and mark dots with a hard pencil.

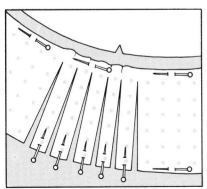

To mark curved area, use either a transfer or graph paper. On the grid, slash between dots to the top row. Align top edge of grid with curve, pin in place, and mark as usual.

Adding smocking to a garment

Smocking can be a most attractive decoration for a garment. It is easiest to apply in areas that have simple, rectangular pattern pieces – a yoke, stand-up collar and cuffs – and it may be used to gather the neckline fullness of a dress for a baby.

TO SMOCK A CUFF

First remove any self-facing on the pattern by cutting along the foldline as in the cuff shown above.

Cut pattern down vertical centre and spread it out on fabric 2½ to 3 times the desired finished width of the smocked area. Pin pattern to fabric. Extend cutting lines, adding a seam allowance at the facing edge. Cut this piece, also replacement facing with corresponding seam allowance.

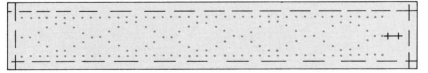

Cut smocking transfer or grid to fit the area you plan to smock. Leave seam allowance free on all sides and stay clear of construction details (such as the buttonhole on the cuff shown). Mark as usual.

Work smocking stitch or desired stitch combinations (pp. 92–95).

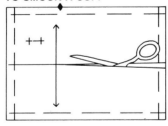

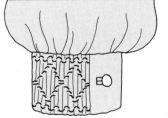

Construct garment according to pattern instructions, attaching smocked piece and replacement facing.

Smocking

Traditional smocking

Traditional smocking is recommended for use by beginners because preparatory gathering into tubes makes the actual smocking stitches easier to work. The rows of running stitches form even, secure pleats, gathering the fabric uniformly. This regulates the tension of the smocking stitches. Preparatory gathering does not, however, determine the width of the completed smocking.

When the running stitches are removed, the area will relax, how much depending on how tightly the smocking is worked. To prepare for gathering, mark the dots on the wrong side of the fabric. Be sure that the grid you mark is appropriate for the stitch you plan to work (see smocking stitches). Do the gathering by hand and work smocking stitches from right side of fabric.

To gather fabric, start thread with a knot at right end of top row of dots. Pick up fabric between dots, making small floats over dots (as shown), or make even running stitches from dot to dot. At end of row, leave a loose thread a few centimetres long. Work all other rows like the first.

Pull all thread ends together at left edge, forming parallel vertical tubes. Pull the threads only tight enough to form even, stable rows. Leave a small space between tubes.

Tie pairs of threads together until all threads are secured at left edge of fabric.

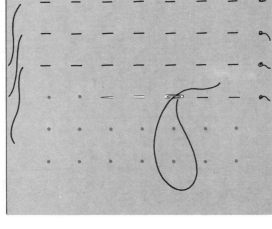 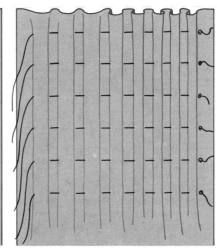 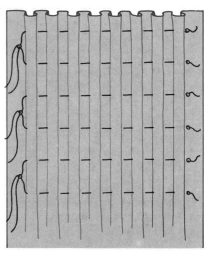

Smocking stitches

The stitch instructions that follow are illustrated in steps for mock smocking. The five stitches on these pages can be worked over any smocking grid. The last two stitches (stitch variations, p. 94) require grids of specific proportions; the grid proportions for these are indicated in the first step of their respective instructions. Be sure to follow these proportions carefully.

All of the stitches can also be worked in traditional smocking. The grid is the same (though the markings are placed on the wrong side of the fabric), and so are the stitch movements. Instead of taking a small stitch at a dot, however, take a stitch at the top of each tube along a row of running stitches. Pick up only a couple of fabric threads at a uniform point on the top of each tube. The last illustration in each sequence shows the stitches worked over the gathered tubes of this method and is intended to help you visualise this way of working.

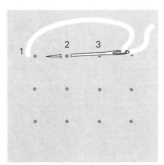 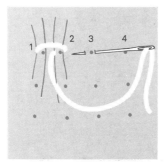 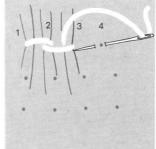 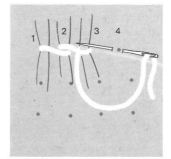 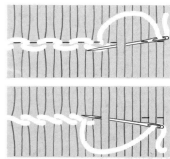

Cable stitch. Work this stitch from left to right. Come up at 1. Then take a small stitch at 2, keeping the thread above the needle.

Pull the thread taut so that points 1 and 2 are drawn together. Take another small stitch at 3, keeping the thread below the needle.

Take a stitch at 4, keeping thread above the needle. Continue this sequence, alternating position of thread above and below the needle.

Stem stitch (also known as outline stitch). Worked as for cable stitch except that the thread is always held below the needle.

Traditional method of working cable and stem stitch. Work across the rows of gathering, taking a small stitch through the top of each tube.

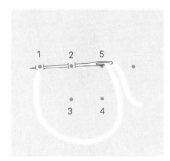
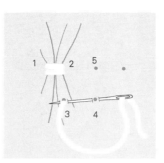
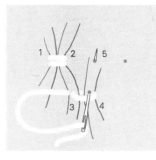
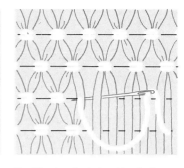

Honeycomb stitch. Work from left to right, with the needle pointing left. Come out at 1, take a small stitch at 2, another at 1. Pull thread taut.

Re-insert the needle at 2, come out at 3 on the row below directly below 2. (This stitch is worked back and forth along two rows of smocking dots.)

Take a small stitch at 4 and another at 3, keeping the needle pointing to the left. Pull the thread taut so that 3 and 4 are drawn together.

Re-insert the needle at 4 and come up in the top row at 5, directly above 4. Point 5 is now point 1 for the start of the next sequence.

Traditional method of working the honeycomb stitch. Work stitch back and forth along two rows of gathering stitches, catching the tube top as shown.

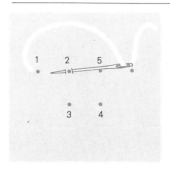
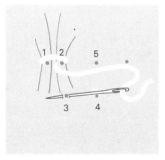
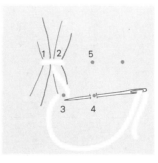
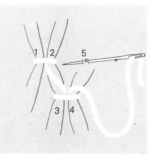
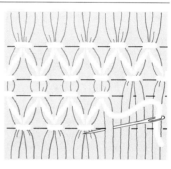

Surface honeycomb stitch. Work left to right, with needle pointing left. Come up at 1 and take a stitch at 2, keeping thread above needle.

Pull thread taut, drawing points 1 and 2 together. Then take a stitch at 3 directly below 2 on the second row of smocking dots.

Take a small stitch at 4, to the right of 3 on second row. Keep thread below needle. Pull thread taut, drawing points 3 and 4 together.

Return to top row and take a stitch at point 5 directly above 4. Point 5 is now point 1 for the beginning of the next sequence.

Traditional method of working surface honeycomb stitch. Work back and forth along two rows of gathering. Note the pattern created by two rows of this stitch.

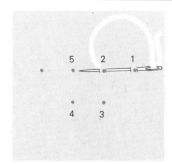
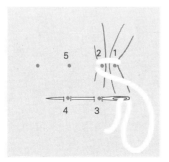
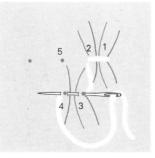
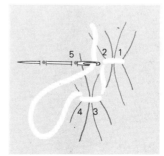
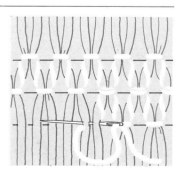

Vandyke stitch. Work from right to left, with needle pointing left. Come up at 2. Take a stitch at 1, another at 2. Keep thread above needle.

Pull the thread taut so that 1 and 2 are drawn together. Then take a stitch at 3 directly below 2 and a stitch at 4 to the left of 3.

Take another stitch at point 3 and at point 4, keeping the thread below the needle. Pull the thread taut so that 3 and 4 are drawn together.

Return to the first row of dots and take a stitch at 5 (point 1 for the next sequence). Repeat Steps 1 to 5 until the row is complete.

For traditional smocking, work Vandyke stitch along two rows of gathering. Note how two rows are worked with the centre stitches overlapping.

Smocking

Stitch variations

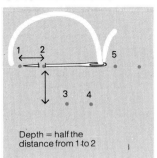

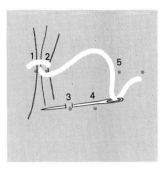

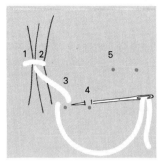

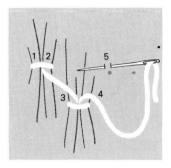

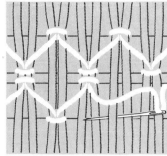

Depth = half the distance from 1 to 2

Wave stitch. Mark dots *only* where stitches will be taken. An all-over grid cannot be used. To work, come up at 1, take a stitch at 2.

Pull thread taut. Take another stitch at 3 below and to the right of 2 in the second row of dots. Wave stitch is worked along two rows of dots.

Keeping thread below needle, take another stitch at 4, directly to the right of 3. Pull thread taut to draw 3 and 4 together.

Return to top row, taking a stitch at point 5. Point 5 is now point 1 for the beginning of the next sequence. Continue pattern to end of row.

For traditional smocking, you can use an all-over grid as the dots do not show once the tubes are drawn up. Work stitch as on left.

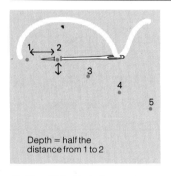

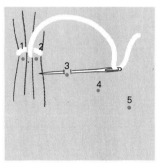

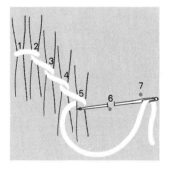

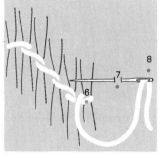

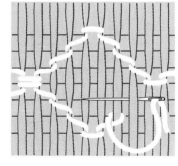

Depth = half the distance from 1 to 2

Trellis stitch. Mark dots as shown. An all-over grid cannot be used. To work, come up at 1, take a stitch at 2. Keep thread above needle.

Pull thread taut. Take another stitch at 3, keeping thread above needle. The distance from 1 to 2 is the same as the distance from 2 to 3.

Take stitches at point 4 and at point 5, still keeping thread above needle. Then take a stitch at 6, this time keeping thread below needle.

Take a stitch up at 7 and continue working diagonally upwards to the top row of dots. Repeat the sequence as needed to complete row.

In traditional smocking this stitch is known as Chevron stitch and can be worked over tubes drawn up in the normal way.

Embellishing stitches

Embroidery stitches are sometimes added to smocking for embellishment. The four stitches shown here (from left to right, lazy daisy, cross stitch, satin stitch and chain stitch) are worked between rows of smocking stitches or in the open areas formed by such stitches as trellis. Work all embellishments over two or more tubes. For detailed instructions, see basic embroidery, pp. 20–51.

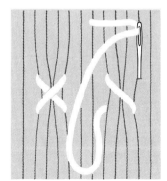

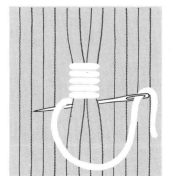

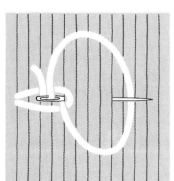

Working stitch combinations

Stitch combinations make the most interesting smocked pieces. If the stitches being combined can all be worked on the same grid, no special treatment is needed. Use mock smocking or the traditional method, as you wish. If, however, the stitches to be combined require different grids, as is true of the combination on the right, smocking must be done by the traditional method, applied in a specific way. The combination on the right is worked as follows: a row of cable stitch, two rows of overlapping wave stitch, and another row of cable, forming the borders; six rows of trellis in the centre; satin stitch embellishments.

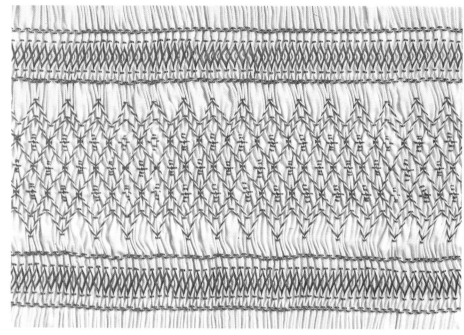

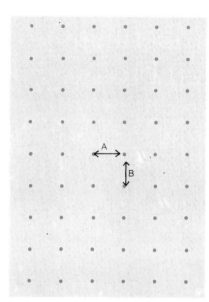

1. Choose a grid for this combination on which the distance between dots and between rows of dots is equal (above, A and B). Mark fabric and gather for traditional smocking.

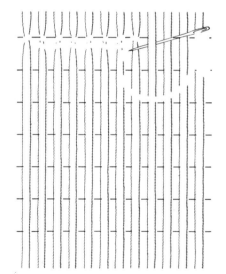

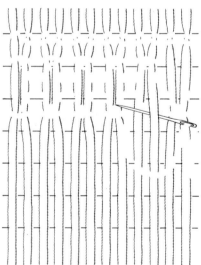

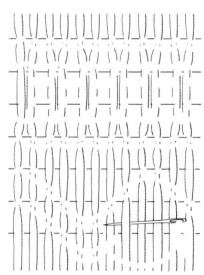

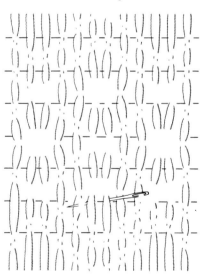

2. To work the stitches in the photographed sample, start at the top row of dots and work a row of cable stitch (refer to p. 92 for detailed instructions) along a row of gathering stitches.

3. Place the wave stitches that follow so that they span 1¼ *times* the distance between rows of gathering stitches. This adjusts the proportions of the grid to those of the stitch.

4. For the trellis stitch that forms the centre pattern, place diagonal stitches to span *half* the distance between gathering rows. This adjusts grid and stitch proportions.

5. Complete six rows of trellis as shown. Repeat border pattern below. Then add embellishments in indicated positions. Satin stitches are used here; for other possibilities, see the facing page.

95

Machine embroidery

Introduction

Though machine embroidery effects are rooted in, and usually named after, traditional hand techniques, each has its own look and style. Except for a few that require a highly sophisticated machine, most of them can be achieved with any efficient zigzag model.

Even the *straight stitch*, the basic stitch on any machine, can produce several embroidery effects (including some free-motion embroidery, see p. 98). Most machine embroidery, however, calls for a *plain zigzag stitch*. Most present-day machines include both a zigzag and a straight stitch. In addition, there is an increasing number of *'automatic' stitches* that can only be worked by a machine equipped with the necessary adjustments or attachments.

Machine embroidery can be worked on almost any type of fabric. If the fabric you choose is lightweight, stitch through paper (which afterwards can be torn away), to prevent puckering. Use machine embroidery thread or normal sewing thread for basic stitching, lurex, pearl cotton or silk twist for special effects. Make sure you know how to use your machine properly; consult the instruction booklet.

Straight stitching

Border motifs can be worked on any straight stitch machine. Use a heavy thread such as silk twist, set stitch length to medium. Mark design on fabric, adjust tension (work a test piece first), and stitch along design lines, pivoting at corners. (To turn corners, see drawings at lower right.)

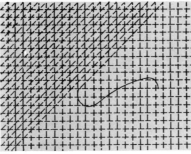

Textured fillings can be worked to resemble hand-embroidered laid work. Use the cross-hatching method shown. Stitch lines horizontally; stitch vertical lines over them. Add diagonal lines on top, following grid formed by the first stitching lines.

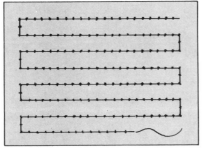

A beaded effect can be created by adjusting top tension so it is slightly tighter than usual. Stitch along design lines. Note how the tightened tension pulls the bobbin thread up, forming tiny beads.

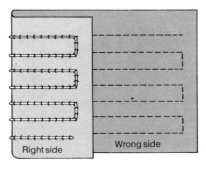

Right side / Wrong side

Mock couching can be achieved with straight stitching. Hand-wind a heavy thread (such as pearl cotton) on bobbin and loosen bobbin tension to accommodate thread. (Not all machines have this adjustment.) Then tighten upper tension. Stitch from wrong side to give couched effect on right side.

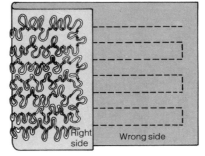

Right side / Wrong side

A looped stitch can be worked simply by adjusting (drastically reducing or completely disengaging) bobbin tension. Wind a heavy thread on bobbin. Then slowly stitch from wrong side of fabric. Small loops will form on right side. (Work a test piece; some machines also need top tension loosened.)

To turn corners, stop machine at corner with needle in fabric. Lift presser foot and turn fabric. Lower foot and continue stitching along design.

Zigzag stitching

Satin stitch, a plain zigzag with a *very short* stitch length, is popular for working along borders and bands. Stitch width can be varied to produce either *wide bands* of stitching or delicate *narrow lines* of satin stitch.

To turn corners, stitch to corner, stopping with needle in fabric at outer edge (for precise point, see drawings, far right). Lift presser foot, turn fabric. Lower foot, resume stitching.

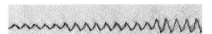

Zigzag filling can be produced with cross-hatching (near right). Work stitches horizontally, cross over these vertically, then diagonally.

A 'wishbone' effect (centre illustration) can be achieved by tightening top tension. Experiment until a satisfactory adjustment is found.

For couching, zigzag over heavy thread or cord. Adjust stitch width to thread thickness; lay thread as you stitch. Thread can match or contrast.

Border design worked in a wide satin stitch.

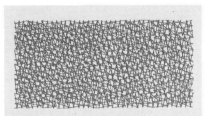

Zigzag filling done with cross-hatching.

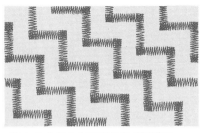

All-over design of narrow satin stitch lines.

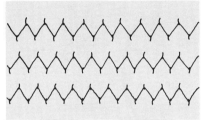

For 'wishbone' effect tighten top tension.

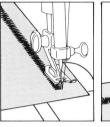

Turn a corner by stopping and pivoting.

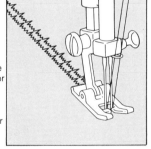

Zigzag couching over heavy thread or cord.

Decorative stitch patterns

Sophisticated machines can work all the straight stitch and zigzag embroidery, and produce fancy patterns as well. Each machine offers its own selection; some of the most common are shown below. Though these stitches are attractive on their own, they can be enhanced in various ways. We show several; these may suggest others. See your instruction booklet for basic stitching information and use of special embroidery feet.

Embroidery over ribbon or braid increases texture and colour impact. Select a stitch of appropriate width, centre the ribbon or braid under the presser foot, and begin stitching. Guide the ribbon carefully so that the embroidery is worked evenly along its length.

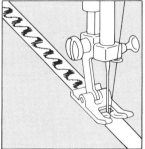

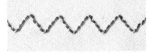

Working with a twin needle produces parallel rows of decorative stitching in one step. Carefully test for stitch width; it must be narrow enough for both needles to clear sides of hole in zigzag throat plate. Use either the same colour thread for both rows, or contrasting colours.

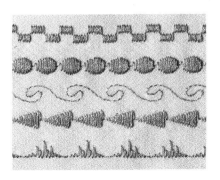

Stitching over a cord is another way to create texture. For the cord, select a contrasting shade of pearl cotton or wool. Keep the cord centred under the presser foot, and guide it carefully as you stitch. There are machine feet with guide holes designed to hold cord in the proper position.

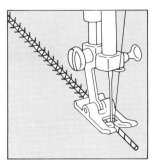

For a heavier stitching line, work a decorative stitch with heavier thread in the bobbin. Fill the bobbin by hand with pearl cotton, loosen bobbin tension (if there is an adjustment), and tighten upper tension slightly. Stitch slowly from the wrong side of work. Use a simple, open stitch pattern.

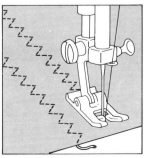

Machine embroidery

Free-motion embroidery

Free-motion embroidery offers unlimited stitching possibilities because fabric motion is not restricted by the presser foot (not used) or the feed dog (either lowered or covered depending on the machine). An embroidery hoop holds the fabric taut and is moved in the desired stitch direction. Control of the hoop movement requires practice. Before beginning any kind of free-motion piece, experiment with thread tension, threads and fabrics to create different effects. Free-motion embroidery can be worked on all machine types. For machine preparation, see below, and read your instruction booklet.

To prepare machine for free-motion work, remove presser foot and its shank. Drop feed dog or cover it with a plate. Set stitch width to 0. Loosen top tension slightly. Be sure needle is a proper size for thread.

Place fabric in embroidery hoop. (Be sure hoop is thin enough to clear presser bar.) Do not use a hoop larger than 20 cm in diameter. Place fabric and backing right side up over larger ring and press inner ring down into outer ring so fabric rests directly on machine bed.

To stitch, lower presser bar to engage upper tension. Holding upper thread taut, turn handwheel towards you to bring up bobbin loop.

Pull bobbin thread up and out so thread ends can be held taut. Hold both top and bobbin threads to the left of the needle as shown.

Take a few stitches to secure threads. Cut off ends as close as possible to stitching.

To manoeuvre hoop, hold it between fingers at edges. Keep elbows down and relaxed. Gently move and guide hoop in the desired direction. Keep machine running at an even, moderate speed. If machine has a speed range, set it at slow until you acquire some expertise. Keep the hoop moving evenly at all times to avoid a pile-up of stitches on the wrong side and possible thread breakage. Length of stitch is controlled by speed at which the work is moved.

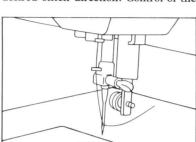
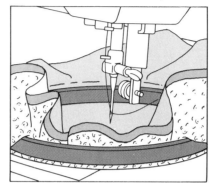
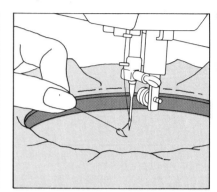
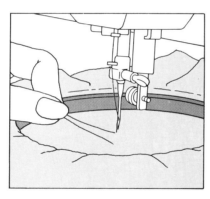
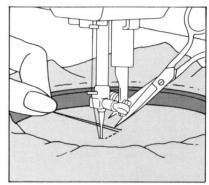
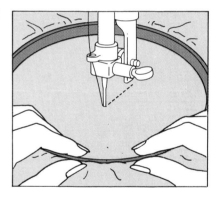

LINE DRAWING

Line drawing is one type of free-motion embroidery. It uses the machine needle to create linear designs. For line drawing, first mark a basic design outline on the fabric. Then improvise the details as you stitch. By altering the machine tension and by using different threads in upper and lower tensions, subtle textures can be created. Heavy threads (pearl cotton or lurex) set in the bobbin also result in interesting surface effects. (Wind heavy bobbin threads by hand, taking care not to stretch them.)

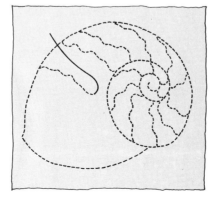

Simple stitch lines can create contour in a design, giving it a three-dimensional look. A shell is an excellent subject for line interpretation. First stitch along marked outline of design. Then stitch interior design lines, improvising as you go.

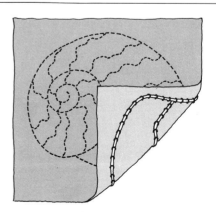

A couched effect can be produced by stitching a design from the wrong side of the fabric, with pearl cotton wound on to the bobbin by hand (do not stretch thread as you wind it). Tighten the upper tension slightly. Move hoop slowly as you work.

SATIN STITCHING

Satin stitch can be worked in free-motion embroidery by setting a zigzag stitch, and moving the frame very slowly, so that the stitches lie close together. The width can be varied during stitching by altering the stitch width lever, but this entails using only one hand to guide the hoop and should only be attempted by an experienced machine embroiderer.

The direction in which the stitches are worked varies the look of the line or filling; hoop movement determines the direction in which the stitches run. Keep the machine in constant motion.

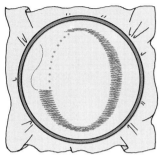

To outline with satin stitch, merely move along design lines. As lines change direction, contour will automatically be formed.

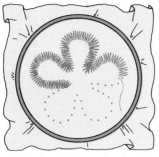

For designs with several parts, rotate hoop continually to work an even line of consistent width along all parts of the design.

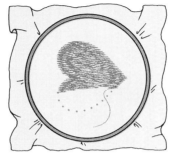

To fill a shape, move hoop slowly from one side to the other and backwards. If you should miss a spot, go back and cover it. Keep the hoop moving.

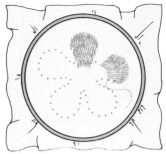

If a design has several parts, fill each part individually, rotating the hoop to move from one part of the design to another.

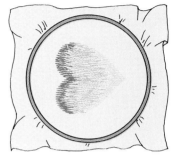

To shade, work several compact rows of satin stitch. Make edges jagged so that the next colour will blend imperceptibly into the previous one.

Machine hemstitching

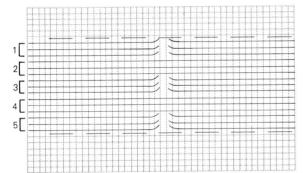

Machine hemstitching requires only a plain zigzag stitch. As in hand hemstitching, threads must be drawn out in a border.

1. Hand-tack upper edge of border. Count off 10 or 15 threads and tack lower edge. Divide threads into 5 groups (2 or 3 threads per group). Cut 1st, 3rd and 5th groups of threads at centre of border, leaving 2nd and 4th intact.

2. Draw out cut threads (groups 1, 3 and 5) to the edges of the border. To stabilise border edges, weave each drawn thread back into wrong side of fabric for 2 cm. Trim the excess thread length.

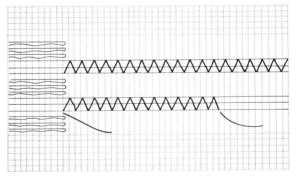

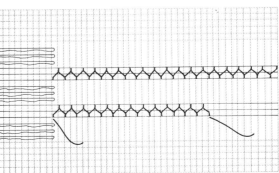

3. Stitch intact threads (groups 2 and 4) within drawn area. Use a normal machine needle, matching or contrasting thread. Hoop is not needed. Set machine to narrow zigzag; stitch over group 2, then group 4. This stitching decorates the border and fastens the threads in each group together.

4. For added texture, tighten the top tension so the zigzag is off-balance (see p. 97). Work this stitch over groups 2 and 4 as for a plain zigzag stitch shown above.

Machine embroidery

Machine cutwork

Machine cutwork can be done on any sewing machine that is equipped for zigzag stitching. It is best to keep designs fairly large; very small and intricate ones can be difficult to work. Stencil designs (also used for hand-embroidered cutwork) work best for machine cutwork. A satin stitch is used to outline the motifs; their centres are then trimmed away close to the stitching. Because of the heavy satin stitching that is worked around the shapes, the fabric needs backing for extra body. A lightweight iron-on interfacing is a good backing choice. Stitch with machine embroidery cotton, number 30 or 50.

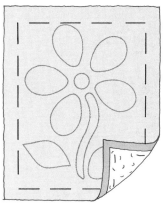

Transfer the design to the right side of the fabric. Cut a piece of interlining large enough to cover the entire design. With wrong sides together, tack the interlining to the fabric.

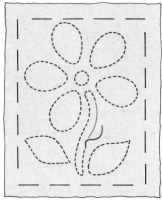

Set the sewing machine to a fine straight stitch (about 7 stitches to the centimetre). Then, working from the right side of the fabric, stitch carefully along the lines of the motif.

Remove tacking and trim away excess interlining, leaving about 3 mm around stitching lines of design. Press interlining that remains; it will provide the necessary body around each shape.

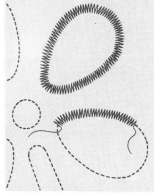

Set the machine for a satin stitch. Work over the straight stitching around each shape. Stop and pivot work often if stitching around sharp corners.

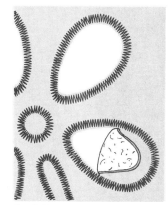

Carefully trim design areas, using a pair of sharp embroidery scissors. Trim as close as possible to satin stitching without cutting the threads. Press entire piece on wrong side.

Machine smocking

A form of mock smocking can be done on any machine. Though machine smocking is similar in appearance to hand smocking, it does not offer the same elasticity, and so is best worked on garments or in areas where elasticity is not needed. Simple smocking can be produced with a straight stitch, a zigzag, or one or more 'automatic' stitches. Fabric to be smocked must first be gathered on several rows of straight machine stitches (select a long stitch length on your machine; about two stitches to the centimetre is appropriate). The mock smocking stitches are then worked using the rows of gathering as a guide.

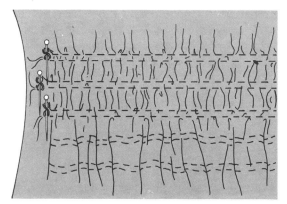

Work rows of gathering stitches in multiples of two, 5 mm apart. Work as many pairs of rows as needed to gather area to be smocked. Space the pairs 1.5 cm apart. Gather to desired width.

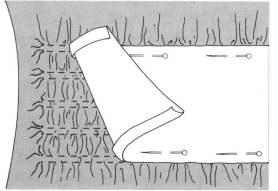

Cut an underlay 3 cm wider than gathered area; fold long edges under 1.5 cm and pin or tack underlay to wrong side of fabric. Test decorative stitches (or plain zigzag) for maximum width of 5 mm.

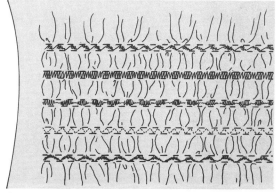

Work 'automatic', plain zigzag or straight stitches between pairs of gathering stitches. Work two rows of stitching when using straight stitch between the pairs of gathering stitches.

Suppliers

JE Beale Plc
26/36 Silver Street
Bedford
MK40 1PE
Telephone: 01234 353292
(needlework materials and canvas)

Handweaver Studio
29 Haroldstone Road
London E17 7AN
Telephone: 0181 521 2281
(embroidery threads)

Harrods Ltd
Knightsbridge
London SW1
Telephone: 0171 730 1234
(needlework materials, canvas and yarns)

John Lewis
Oxford Street
London W1
Telephone: 0171 629 7711
(needlework materials)

Mace & Nairn
89 Crane Street
Salisbury
Wilts
Telephone: 01722 336903
(embroidery materials)

Christine Riley's Embroidery Shop
53 Barclay Street
Stonehaven
Kincardineshire
AB3 2AR
Telephone: 01569 763238
(needlework materials)

Royal School of Needlework
Apartment 12A
Hampton Court Palace
East Molesey
Surrey
KT8 9AU
Telephone: 0181 943 1432
(needlework materials, canvas, frames, needles, yarns)

Specialist Crafts Ltd
PO Box 247
Leicester
LE1 9QS
Telephone: 01533 510405
(needlework supplies)

Spinning Jenny
Market Place
Masham
Ripon
N Yorks
Telephone: 01765 689351
(embroidery materials)

Photographic credit
page 10 Flower and bird design.
The Bagshaws of St Lucia Ltd.
Silk-screen bamboo-print wallpaper,
Janovic/Plaza.

Index